stea

devotions for baseball fans

HUGH POLAND

JUDSON PRESS

PUBLISHERS SINCE 1824

VALLEY FORGE

steal away: devotions for baseball fans
© 2006 by Judson Press, Valley Forge, PA 19482-0851
All rights reserved.

Unless otherwise noted, Bible quotations in this volume are from The HOLY BIBLE: *New International Version* (NIV), copyright © 1973, 1978, 1984. Used by permission of Zondervan.

Bible quotations in this volume marked NKJV are from The New King James Version. Copyright © 1972, 1984 by Thomas Nelson Inc. Bible quotations in this volume marked NRSV are from the New Revised Standard Version of the Bible, copyright © 1989 by the Division of Christian Education of the National Council of the Churches of Christ in the United States of America. Used by permission. All rights reserved.

Bible quotations in this volume marked NLT are from the *Holy Bible*, New Living Translation, copyright © 1996. Used by permission of Tyndale House Publishers, Inc., Wheaton, IL 60189. All rights reserved.

Steal away : devotions for baseball fans / Hugh Poland. —1st ed.   p. cm.
Includes bibliographical references.   ISBN 0-8170-1491-8 (alk. paper)
1. Christian life. 2. Baseball fans—Religious life. 3. Baseball—Religious life—Christianity. I. Title.
BV4501.3.P65 2006   424'.68—dc22   2005033963

Printed in the U.S.A.
Second Edition, 2007.

The voice of Your thunder was in the whirlwind;
The lightnings lit up the world;
The earth trembled and shook.
—Psalm 77:18, NKJV

Steal away, steal away,
Steal away to Jesus!
Steal away, steal away home,
I ain't got long to stay here.
My Lord calls me;
He calls me by thunder;
The Trumpet sounds within my soul,
I ain't got long to stay here.
—African American spiritual

For Karen

contents

foreword

GROWING UP IN PANAMA, I DREAMED OF PLAYING PROFESSIONAL BASEBALL THOUGH the odds were stacked against me. My first "glove" was made from cardboard. When I was twenty years old, word spread that a scout from the New York Yankees was coming to Panama. He was not coming to see me; the Yankees had never heard of me. A friend encouraged me to try out, and I did. The scout liked what he saw, and eventually I was drafted by the Yankees. Today, I am overwhelmingly grateful for the opportunity I have had to fulfill the dream of playing the sport I love.

The light of my faith brings everything into perspective. The visit from the scout was not something I had planned or expected. This is one of the reasons for my testimony that every step of my life has been ordered by my Lord and Savior, Jesus Christ. Therefore everything I have accomplished I owe to him.

I sense in *Steal Away* a familiar passion both for baseball and for following Christ. Hugh Poland provides readers with interesting and little known facts and stories about many of the "heroes" of the game—past and present. His purpose, however, is to help readers grow in their understanding of and commitment to Jesus Christ. I hope and believe that his words will bless you and draw you nearer to Jesus, the greatest hero of all time.   **—Mariano Rivera**

preface

BASEBALL IS NEVER MENTIONED IN THE SCRIPTURES, THOSE HAVING BEEN WRITten long before the Cartwrights and Spaldings and others known only to God helped evolve the game. But baseball is story, and as such it has much in common with Jesus' teaching method. Jesus taught in parables, imaginative stories of commonplace events that were filled with wonderful truth.

The word *parable* comes from the Greek, meaning "to cast alongside of." Imagine tossing a simple story next to a big idea. The interaction between the two is what parables are about. Following the pattern of Jewish teachers of the day, Jesus used parables to teach truths, especially truths of the kingdom of God. In essence Jesus was saying, "So you think you know what the kingdom is like? Listen to this story and then see what you think." In a sense Jesus was playing a game of catch with his audiences—"See if you can catch this one"—and challenging them to think differently, to conceive of old ideas in new ways.

I don't remember when I first noticed the game of baseball. I do remember my first pack of baseball cards, my first home run over the fence in the backyard, my first uniform, and the first major-league game I ever attended. I also remember that I placed my faith in Christ at the tender age of nine, and I knew that God loved me and would never leave me.

But it took twenty more years for me to begin to see the parables in the game that speak so strongly of redemption, of justice, of hope and forgiveness, of faithfulness and perseverance. Perhaps that is because I live in such a busy age. There is little time for doubleheaders anymore. I find myself shunning the "businessperson's special" afternoon game so I can get a little more work done. This may not fall into the category of breaking the Ten Commandments, but does it really do my soul any good to work harder while life is rapidly passing by?

When we are too busy for God, we are busier than God wants us to be. The purpose of this book is to help the reader "steal away" to God by recounting stories from the greatest game ever played and making connections with scriptural truths. The Bible is a dangerous book—if you read it, it will change your life. Combined with prayer, even the busiest fan will find his or her heart growing warm toward the things of God as the long winter melts into spring and we hear those magical words again: "Pitchers and catchers report . . ."

Like baseball, writing is a team sport. Of the current and former players, players' wives, coaches, and umpires I interviewed, many were especially helpful, including Sal Bando, Betty Barbary, Ted Barrett, John Boccabella, Bernie Carbo, Alvin Dark, Tom Griffin, Randy Harling, Ed Herrmann, Frank Minton, and Jim Sundberg. I also have to thank a dear friend, Dale Seibert. From the moment I met him, he was retelling old baseball stories and bolstering me with the greatest encouragement in Christ a friend could ever have.

All first-time authors should have editors like Randy Frame and Cassandra Williams of Judson Press. They have both encouraged me to swing for the fences.

My wife, Karen, and my three daughters, Kayse, Jayme, and Ally, have endured a lot of evenings having Dad at the computer or at the library. I have no greater joy than to know that my bases are loaded and that Jesus has done what it takes to make sure you all will arrive safely home someday.

C'mon, let's play catch. . . .

SPRING TRAINING

Let us acknowledge the LORD*;*
let us press on to acknowledge him.
As surely as the sun rises,
he will appear;
he will come to us like the winter rains,
like the spring rains that water the earth.
—Hosea 6:3

"That's the true harbinger of spring, not crocuses or swallows returning to Capistrano, but the sound of a bat on the ball."[1]
—Bill Veeck, former owner of the Chicago White Sox

"Any tree in America would gladly give its life for the glory of a day at home plate."[2]
—Congressman Richard H. Durbin

scout's honor

Jesus entered Jericho and was passing through. A man was there by the name of Zacchaeus; he was a chief tax collector and was wealthy. He wanted to see who Jesus was, but being a short man he could not, because of the crowd. So he ran ahead and climbed a sycamore-fig tree to see him, since Jesus was coming that way.

When Jesus reached the spot, he looked up and said to him, "Zacchaeus, come down immediately. I must stay at your house today." So he came down at once and welcomed him gladly.

All the people saw this and began to mutter, "He has gone to be the guest of a 'sinner.'"

But Zacchaeus stood up and said to the Lord, "Look, Lord! Here and now I give half of my possessions to the poor, and if I have cheated anybody out of anything, I will pay back four times the amount."

Jesus said, "Today salvation has come to this house, because this man, too, is a son of Abraham. For the Son of Man came to seek and to save what was lost."
—Luke 19:1-10

"When I was a small boy in Kansas, a friend of mine and I went fishing. . . . I told him I wanted to be a real major league baseball player, a genuine professional like Honus Wagner. My friend said that he'd like to be President of the United States. Neither of us got our wish."[1]
—Dwight D. Eisenhower, 34th president of the United States

WITHIN BASEBALL, THERE IS ONE POSITION THAT IS CRITICAL TO THE SUCCESS of a team: the "bird dog," or baseball scout. Great players are often found in the sticks and hollers and places not found on the map, and the scout has a passion to track them down and report on their potential. While fans remember their favorite players, in most instances they never remember the name of the scout who first discovered the player. In fact, typing "Famous Baseball Scouts" into an Internet search engine doesn't even register one hit. The names of Tom Greenwade and Dewey Griggs don't ring a bell, but the players they signed sure do: Mickey Mantle and Hank Aaron.

The 17-year-old Mantle could have become a Cleveland Indian, not a New York Yankee. He was a shortstop and had not initially been on Tom Greenwade's list of players to watch. Another scout had already seen Mantle, but having heard that he had been injured playing football, the scout recommended to the Cleveland Indians that Mantle not be signed. Greenwade had gone to a game to watch another player, but he saw some potential in Mantle and he recommended the Yankees sign him after he finished high school.

Dewey Griggs saw in Aaron a soft-spoken young man who hadn't even played baseball in high school. On top of that, Aaron batted cross-handed. Yet the experienced scout perceived that Aaron had the makings of a major-league player. Yet even Griggs couldn't have known that Aaron would go on to become baseball's all-time home-run king.

In 1954 Brooklyn Dodgers scouts signed two left-handed pitchers. After three years, one had a winning record, and one had a losing record, causing some in the organization to give up on him. Yet the first never made it to the majors, and the second went on to the Hall of Fame. How can it be?

"They were looking for left-handed pitchers," says Frank Minton, now a Southern Baptist minister. "My twin brother and I were the leaders of our high school team, and there were plenty of scouts in the stands to see us play. A couple of teams showed interest in me, but when the Dodgers wanted to sign us both, well, that clinched the deal. They told me they had me on track to break into the majors by my sixth year in baseball. But after three years I sensed God calling me into the ministry, so I retired with a 37–17 W–L record and became a pastor."[2]

The other southpaw, the one with the losing record after three years? That player was none other than Sandy Koufax. Koufax went on to become one of the most dominating left-handers of all time, retiring with a remarkable 165–87 W–L record.

POTENTIAL. It's what the scouts saw in Mickey, Hank, Frank, and even Sandy. It's also what Jesus saw in Zacchaeus, a man who, because of his size, could get lost in a crowd with ease. If not for the fact that people despised Zacchaeus because he was a cheat and a tax collector working in an injust system, he would never have been noticed at all. Surely this man would not have made a good follower of Jesus.

But Jesus didn't merely cast a glance his way. He deliberately reached out to Zacchaeus. Out of all the people gathered around that tree, Jesus spoke to Zacchaeus and announced his intentions to eat a meal with him. Jesus saw Zacchaeus not for who he *was*, but for who he *could* be if he began to follow the Lord. The good news is that Jesus looks at all of us the same way—not for who we've been, but for who we have the *potential* to be.

winning pitch: Chances are that person you've snubbed or written off is just the person God wants you to look at again. The disciples were "unschooled, ordinary men" (Acts 4:13), David was the youngest and smallest of his brothers (1 Samuel 16:7-13), and Amos was a simple shepherd and farmer (Amos 7:14-15), but the Lord saw the potential in each of them and used them for great things. Dare to see the people around you through God's eyes—the possibilities for their lives will come out as they respond to the love you show them.

hitting the cutoff man

Therefore, rid yourselves of all malice and all deceit, hypocrisy, envy, and slander of every kind. Like newborn babies, crave pure spiritual milk, so that by it you may grow up in your salvation, now that you have tasted that the Lord is good.
—1 Peter 2:1-3

"Catching a fly ball is a pleasure. But knowing what to do with it after you catch it is a business."[1]
—Tommy Henrich, Yankees outfielder

SPRING TRAINING IS A TIME TO EVALUATE THE TALENT IN A BALL CLUB AND address the fundamentals of the game. Players practice the "little things" that matter most. The team learns the signs for bunt, steal, and hit-and-run. Fielders learn how to position themselves, how to hit the cutoff man, how to execute a rundown, and how to turn the double play. The repetition can be boring, but according to Alvin Dark, the fundamentals are critical.

Dark should know. He played the game and managed for a total of 27 years. "As a fielder, you have to have it in your mind where you are at all times, where you will run, and where you will throw the ball," he says. "You can't decide these things on the spur of the moment. These fundamentals must be learned before the game starts."

Dark was Rookie of the Year as a shortstop with the Boston Braves in 1948, was selected to the All-Star game three times, and believes he was born to play the game. "Ever since I was a kid, I wanted to be a ballplayer. My father was a semi-pro baseball player, and my brother played in the minor leagues. I had accepted Christ into my life at age 11, and the older I got the more I realized God was indeed preparing my life to be a baseball player.

"When I was a boy, I had good coaches that helped me keep my focus and learn the fundamentals of the game at an early age," Dark reminisces. "A person can't be a successful baseball player without the fundamentals of the game." Once he made the majors, Dark was a real spark plug on the teams he played on. The scrappy infielder was a real pest to opposing pitchers, hitting over .300 four times in his career and proving difficult to strike out.

After his playing days were over, he became a manager. In 1960 the Giants had been a mediocre team, but in 1961 Dark was named the skipper. "I went into spring training that year determined to teach those same fundamentals I had learned, and it paid off. We won the pennant in 1962," he says. In 1971

Dark recommitted his life to the Lord, and in 1974 he found himself managing the defending champion Oakland A's. The team was notorious for its execution of the fundamentals, and they went on to win a third consecutive World Series. "Good pitching is fundamental, too," says Dark. "When you can run Jim Hunter, Ken Holtzman, and Vida Blue out there pretty regularly, and have Rollie Fingers as the closer, it's not too hard to be successful.

"At the same time they were executing the fundamentals *on* the field, they were learning about the fundamentals of life *off* the field," says Dark, known for his faith. "We started an optional chapel service for the team, and over the course of the season 14 men came to know Christ. Many realized their lives were not in order, that something was missing, and one by one they began to consider what God's Word says about living. Even today, I still hear from players on that team, telling me what a difference those chapel services made in their lives."[2]

What is true for fundamentals in baseball is also true in life. A Christian cannot live life the way God meant it to be lived without practicing the fundamentals of the faith, namely studying the Word of God and engaging in prayer. Something is missing at the center of the human heart when the One who is the Living Word is not enthroned there.

winning pitch: If you've never had a daily time alone with God, begin by setting aside ten minutes each day. Make an appointment that you will not break, and ask someone else to help keep you accountable. Then begin to read a few verses each day, perhaps beginning in the book of Mark or the Psalms. Spend some time reflecting on the passage, using the "SPACE" acrostic:

Is there a SIN for me to confess?

Is there a PROMISE for me to claim?

Is there an ATTITUDE for me to change?

Is there a CHARACTER for me to develop?

Is there an EXAMPLE for me to follow?

Close in prayer, asking God to help you develop the fundamentals of your faith.

know the signs

As Jesus was sitting on the Mount of Olives, the disciples came to him privately. "Tell us," they said, "when will this happen, and what will be the sign of your coming and of the end of the age?"

Jesus answered: "Watch out that no one deceives you. For many will come in my name, claiming, 'I am the Christ,' and will deceive many."
—Matthew 24:3-5

"I don't care what [directions] the manager gave to me. They could be tough. My objective was to give them to the players with the easiest set of signs I could have. It's hard enough to hit off a 95 mile-per-hour fastball without having to think, 'What was that?'"[1]
—Don Zimmer, New York Yankees third base coach

NEXT TIME YOU'RE AT A BALL GAME, TAKE A LOOK AT THE THIRD BASE COACH between pitches. He pats himself and scratches his nose so much you'd think he needs mosquito repellent. Look into the dugout to see the manager or bench coach making unusual movements, waving scorecards, or touching the bill of his cap. Watch the catcher wiggle his hand and hold down one finger to the pitcher, who nods in agreement and, in a tradition time-honored since Little League, throws a fastball instead of a curve.

These aren't just strange tics—these are the very strategy of the game, the signs. And hundreds of signs are given every game, from indicating types of pitches to locating fielders to calling for a squeeze play.

"I don't think you could play without signs," says baseball historian Paul Dickson, author of the book *The Hidden Language of Baseball.* "It would be chaotic. The manager would have no way to communicate. The pitcher would be doing anything he wanted. There would be no coordination, no battery as we know it."[2]

When players understand the signs, the game goes along smoothly. But sometimes, in the heat of battle, a player gets mixed up on the signals. The results can be hilarious.

The Dodgers used to signal for a squeeze play by having the third base coach, Leo Durocher, call out to the runner on third by his last name. One day, slugger Frank Howard reached third, and the play was on. Durocher leaned over from the third base coaching box and said, "OK, stay awake, Howard." Howard, oblivious to what was going on, gave his coach a warm smile and said, "Aw, Leo, you know you can call me Frank."[3]

Boston had a more complicated process of signs based on how many times a coach would touch himself. Base runners would add or subtract the signs and know what to do.

One night outfielder Bernie Carbo was caught stealing, and manager Darrell Johnson asked Carbo to clarify what sign he thought he had seen that would make him run.

"Two plus two," Carbo replied.

"That's four—the take sign," said Johnson. "The steal sign is five."

Carbo replied, "I added wrong."[4]

Former Dodger first baseman Dick Stuart was so inept at picking up signs that third base coach Preston Gomez once gave him a steal sign simply by moving his arms in a running motion and pointing to second base.

A follower of Christ must know the signs and what they mean. The disciples wanted to know how they would recognize Jesus when he came again. What would be the sign?

Jesus spoke of many signs in Matthew 24–25. Various theories are held by many scholars about the second coming of Christ, but one sign in particular seems to stand out. Matthew 24:26-27 says: "So if anyone tells you, 'There he is, out in the desert,' do not go out; or, 'Here he is, in the inner rooms,' do not believe it. For as lightning that comes from the east is visible even in the west, so will be the coming of the Son of Man." In other words, the second coming of Christ will be a fantastic, visible event, and it will come quickly.

Think of it: When Jesus comes again, he won't have to go door to door, pass out pamphlets, or take out an ad in the paper to tell you he's back. There will be no mistaking him for someone else. His return will be swift, and it will be obvious. He will not slowly rise to power as a political figure somewhere here on earth. Instead, he will return on the clouds, with power and great glory (see Daniel 7:13-14).

Don't be fooled. There will be many impostors in the last days. A true teammate of Jesus will know the signs and won't get caught on a pick-off play.

winning pitch: Even if you could have a blueprint of your future, it would probably be a hindrance to your faith. What is most important is not that we know some sort of prophetic timetable, but that we understand how we are to live while we are waiting for Jesus to come back. After all, if even Jesus does not know when his Father will send him to earth a second time (Mark 13:32-33), then it will do us no good to speculate regarding dates and times. Just seek to live each day as if the second coming of Christ could be today!

sacrifice play

Do nothing out of selfish ambition or vain conceit, but in humility consider others better than yourselves. Each of you should look not only to your own interests, but also to the interests of others.
Your attitude should be the same as that of Christ Jesus:
Who, being in very nature God,
did not consider equality with God something to be grasped,
but made himself nothing,
taking the very nature of a servant,
being made in human likeness.
And being found in appearance as a man,
he humbled himself
and became obedient to death—
even death on a cross!
Therefore God exalted him to the highest place
and gave him the name that is above every name,
that at the name of Jesus every knee should bow,

in heaven and on earth and under the earth,
and every tongue confess that Jesus Christ is Lord,
to the glory of God the Father.
—Philippians 2:3-11

"More important than all else, let us remember that 'the means of grace and the hope of glory' trace back exactly to the great sacrifice play—the Good Player, for each of us, when the Good Manager so ordered, placed each of us in a better scoring position, in a certain three-hour game, on a certain Friday, on a certain field named Calvary."[1]
—Red Barber, Hall of Fame baseball announcer

"Everybody judges players different. I judge a player by what he does for his ball club and not by what he does for himself. I think the name of the game is self-sacrifice."[2]
—Billy Martin, manager

ONE OF THE KEY PLAYERS ON THE OAKLAND A'S CHAMPIONSHIP TEAMS OF THE early 1970s was third baseman and team captain Sal Bando. Bando was considered a natural leader, the glue of the infield, a powerful hitter, and was named to the American League All-Star Team on four different occasions.

But something was still missing. In 1974, when Alvin Dark was named as manager of the A's, a chapel service was started for the team. Even though he had been raised in a religious home, Bando sensed there was something more to life, and so he began to attend chapel regularly. In August 1975 Bando made a full-fledged commitment of his life to Christ and has continued in his commitment to this very day. In fact, God took the leadership skills Bando showed on the field and began to use him as a leader off the field.

"On or off the field, I think you have to realize you are no better than the next guy," Bando says. "If you want respect as a leader, you have to play with a single purpose of winning, and not so much for your own self-gratification. My desire to win the game was always foremost, compared to how well I played."

On a team full of colorful characters who pushed baseball, team spirit, and even fashion to a new level, Bando remained a quiet leader.

"I've always been a leader, but it took me awhile to realize there are many things I cannot do on my own, things that I have to turn over to the Lord. I wasn't the best player on the team, but I was never afraid to be competitive, and I wasn't afraid to step forward and speak up at times. Unfortunately, at one point I was making baseball my God. I am so thankful that in spite of that, God has been so gracious to me."[3]

To sacrifice is to forfeit something highly valued for the sake of something that is considered to have a greater value or claim. In baseball, a batter will sacrifice a bunt for the sake of moving a runner over into scoring position, thus giving his team a chance to score.

God was so gracious to us, as Bando says, by sacrificing his Son for our sins. In doing so the Lord of the universe taught us that the best way to lead is by giving up our own selfish desires for the good of others. Jesus could have clung to his riches in heaven—untold wealth that was rightfully his. Instead, he made himself "nothing" and humbled himself even to the point of death on a cross. And he calls his followers to imitate him with unselfish acts of love and devotion.

Baseball isn't the only place where sacrifice is appreciated. Inside the kingdom of God, it is an everyday occurrence.

winning pitch: How can you put someone above yourself today? How about doing a random act of kindness for someone? Even better, do something good for someone today without his or her knowing it. Leave a gift in someone's chair at work without signing your name. Put a special book on someone's doorstep without ringing the bell. Take flowers to a retirement home and simply go up to the first resident you see and hand them over. Your heavenly Father sees what is done in secret and will reward you (Matthew 6:4).

laughter at vinegar bend

A cheerful heart is good medicine,
but a crushed spirit dries up the bones.
—Proverbs 17:22

"Shucks, those guys [in the Cuban Winter League] couldn't understand the language I was pitching to them in. That's why I struck out so many."[1]
—Vinegar Bend Mizell, pitcher, 1952–1962

THE ABILITY TO BE ABLE TO LAUGH AT YOURSELF IS A STRONG TRAIT IN A SPIRItually healthy person. Take the case of Wilmer "Vinegar Bend" Mizell.

Before there was Roger Clemens or Randy Johnson, before there was Nolan Ryan or Sandy Koufax, there was Wilmer Mizell. Mizell hailed from the rural town of Vinegar Bend, Alabama, and a St. Louis Cardinals front office desperate to sell tickets nicknamed him after his hometown. Describing living conditions in the humble setting, Mizell once said, "One day a fire started in the bathroom, but we were able to put it out before it reached the house." He had an incredibly live fastball and was deemed by St. Louis faithful to be the second coming of Dizzy Dean.

After spending time in the minors, notably as the ace of the 1951 Houston Buffs Texas League championship team, he was called up to the Cardinals. He spent seven years with the St. Louis team before being traded to the Pirates in the middle of the 1960 season, and went 13-5 down the stretch for a team that defeated the Yankees in one of the most dramatic World Series ever. Mizell finished up his career with the Mets in 1962. He later became a member of the U.S. House of Representatives, serving three terms. A dedicated Christian on and off the field, he championed the cause of the *Jesus* film for Campus Crusade until his death.

Mizell once humorously spoke of his effort as the doomed starter in game three of the 1960 World Series. In front of 70,000 fans at Yankee Stadium, he retired only one batter and gave up five runs. "If people tuned in to the game late on the radio or TV, they missed me completely!" he once said self-deprecatingly. But he still wore his World Series ring with pride, having pitched well during the regular season for the Bucs, who went on to defeat the Yankees four games to three.

His delivery was definitely old school. With a slow, arching windup, Mizell would rear back with his leg kicked high and his pitching hand oh-so-close to the mound. Then he would bring the ball over the top and blow it by a hitter. When asked about his delivery, Mizell would reply with a twinkle in his eye, "Not only did I occasionally touch the mound with my pitching hand, sometimes I would actually knock the ball out of my hand before I could deliver it to the plate!"[2]

One might think a Christian, a Congressman, and a competitive person would be very serious minded and have little reason to laugh, but that's not the case. Mizell realized what many others have not discovered: A cheerful heart is like a good medicine. Only Christians can really laugh with a security—we know the end of the story! We know how it all turns out. Jesus wins in the end. Our enemy is defeated once and for all. Our sins are forgiven, our tears are wiped dry, and our future is glorious.

So go ahead and laugh. Snicker at yourself when the ball gets knocked out of your hand. Giggle when you test gravity by dropping something. Smile when you trip over a crack in the sidewalk. Guffaw with glee when you get the date wrong. Tell a joke on yourself in a crowd. Those around you will appreciate that you don't take yourself too seriously. Your ability to laugh also gives them hope for the next time they knock the ball out of their own hand.

winning pitch: Memorize Proverbs 17:22 and ask a trusted friend to gently remind you when you're taking yourself too seriously.

prayer locker

This is the confidence we have in approaching God: that if we ask anything according to his will, he hears us. And if we know that he hears us—whatever we ask—we know that we have what we asked of him.
—1 John 5:14-15

"The main thing is prayer. Through spending time getting to know God's heart I can deal with things. I want to have the heart of Jesus and that intimacy with Him. So you've got to stay in prayer."[1]
—Harold Reynolds, All-Star infielder, 1983–1994, and ESPN baseball analyst, when asked how he deals with the highs and lows of professional baseball

SOMETIMES THERE IS CONFUSION ABOUT THE MYSTERY OF PRAYER. DOES GOD hear our prayers? Does he really answer them? Can I receive whatever I ask for? Tom Griffin was *The Sporting News* Rookie Pitcher of the Year in 1969. That year he went 11–10 with 200 strikeouts for a Houston Astros team that celebrated its first non-losing season ever. But Griffin discovered that sucess is fleeting. By 1972 he was reporting to spring training with arm problems and fighting just to make the rotation.

"It was during that spring training that I heard the testimony of another one of our pitchers, Dave Roberts. At first I wasn't sure what to think about it, but I became convinced that I needed a relationship with God, too, so I committed my life to Christ at that time," says Griffin.

"Now in spring training, pitchers are all trying to get their arms in shape, and so you start out slow. Nobody pitches nine innings the first day. You typically start out with one, then two, then the equivalent of three innings, then more if your arm feels good. I was trying to make the team as a starter, not a reliever, and was in competition with several other pitchers.

"So my experience with Christ was real fresh when I went to the mound in an exhibition game against the Twins in Orlando. It suddenly occurred to me before the game that, well, maybe I should pray," says Griffin. "So I sat at my locker and looked around to make sure no one was watching me, and I prayed something like, 'Uh, Lord, you probably know I'm a Christian now, and I'm asking you to help me in today's game. Lord, I want to pitch three innings, give up no hits, no runs, no walks, and strike out three.

"Lo and behold, I went out to the mound and did exactly that! So I thought to myself, 'This Christianity stuff is great! I'm gonna be the greatest pitcher ever!'

"So several days later I'm scheduled to start another game against the Phillies in Clearwater. Again I prayed in front of my locker, looking over my shoulder to make sure no one saw me. This time I asked the Lord for five innings, no hits, no runs, no walks, and to be able to strike out five.

"Well, I only lasted one-third of an inning. I gave up several hits, runs, walks, and I even hit batters. It was one of the worst days I ever had as a professional.

"I quickly realized that this Christianity thing wasn't going to work out the way I thought it would. It wasn't long after that when I came upon Philippians 4:6-7, which says, 'Do not be anxious about anything, but in everything, by prayer and petition, with thanksgiving, present your requests to God. And the peace of God, which transcends all understanding, will guard your hearts and your minds in Christ Jesus.'

"For the first time ever, I experienced God's peace. It was a peace that surpassed anything I had ever experienced before, and it was in spite of the bad outing I'd had. I realized that I had given God my best, and that was all that mattered. I was content to leave the rest up to him."[2]

Prayer is not the Christian version of a spiritual slot machine. Prayer isn't a matter of speaking magical words into the air, pulling down the arm of God's sovereignty, and seeing a jackpot of whatever you ask for spilling out into your lap. Prayer is not a formula for getting what *we* want; it's a way of communicating to God and of seeking to know and desire what God wants.

winning pitch: Get into your locker or seek out a quiet space today. Dedicate some time in prayer to seek God's will for your life. Remember, God listens to your heart more than your tongue. So if you're not sure how to pray, begin by asking for the desires of your heart to be molded to match the will of God. You can then pray in honesty, telling God that you commit to his will in whatever matters are on your mind, even if it means that you don't get the particular answer you want to hear at the moment.

OPENING DAY

Do you not know that in a race all the runners run, but only one gets the prize? Run in such a way as to get the prize. Everyone who competes in the games goes into strict training. They do it to get a crown that will not last; but we do it to get a crown that will last forever. Therefore I do not run like a man running aimlessly; I do not fight like a man beating the air. No, I beat my body and make it my slave so that after I have preached to others, I myself will not be disqualified for the prize.
—1 Corinthians 9:24-27

"You always get a special kick on opening day, no matter how many you go through. You look forward to it like a birthday party when you're a kid. You think something wonderful is going to happen."[1]
—Joe DiMaggio, Yankees outfielder, 1936–1951

the heart of a pee wee

If you have any encouragement from being united with Christ, if any comfort from his love, if any fellowship with the Spirit, if any tenderness and compassion, then make my joy complete by being like-minded, having the same love, being one in spirit and purpose.
—Philippians 2:1-2

"If I had my career to play over, one thing I'd do differently is swing more. Those 1,200 walks I got—nobody remembers them."[1]
—Pee Wee Reese, Dodgers shortstop, 1940–1958

IN 1947 THE WORLD WAS A VERY DIFFERENT PLACE. CIVIL RIGHTS ACTS WERE STILL several years on the horizon, and major-league baseball had existed for many years with its racial inequalities. When Jackie Robinson first came up to the Dodgers, not only did fans and players in other cities despise him, but even several of his own teammates who were against his becoming a Dodger.

At one point there was a petition circulating inside the clubhouse that several players had signed in an effort to force Robinson out. But this protest was short-lived when the captain of the Dodgers, Harold "Pee Wee" Reese, refused to sign it.

Pee Wee's size contributed to his nickname, but he always claimed that he got the moniker as a young marbles champion, shooting "pee wees." The nickname stuck, but it in no way described the size of his heart or his ability. A smooth fielder, he became the premier shortstop of his era, an All-Star each year from 1947 to 1954. He was also a great leadoff hitter, leading the National League in walks (104) in 1947, in runs scored (132) in 1949, and in stolen bases (30) in 1952. He was also noted for his clutch hitting and excellent bat control. Reese's highest average was .309 in 1954.

But it's what Reese did before games that has become his enduring legacy.

When the Dodgers would take the field in the first inning, Jackie Robinson would become the object of fierce taunting and catcalls that would have broken a lesser man. But on several occasions, Reese would calmly walk over to Robinson and put his arm around his shoulder, demonstrating to all that he was Robinson's teammate and friend, accepting him into the fold even though he had a different skin color. His act showed the world that he and Robinson were equals.

Robinson also received many death-threat letters before games. In one particular instance, the Ku Klux Klan threatened to shoot him during the game if he showed up on the field.

That evening, while warming up, Pee Wee's poise, wit, and courage came out again. Playing toss with teammates alongside Jackie, Reese said jokingly, "Jackie, get away from me, will you? That guy might be a bad shot!"

The two players shared a laugh and played the entire game. Their hearts were so full of love and admiration for each other and for the wonderful game they played that there was no room for fear.

Years later, Pee Wee's humility was still shining. "Just don't make me out to be a hero. It took no courage to do what I did," he said in an interview. "Jackie had the courage. If it had been me, a white man, trying to be the only one in the black leagues, I couldn't have done it. What he had to endure, the criticism, the catcalls—I wouldn't have had the courage."[2]

A short time after the death of Jesus, a vicious opponent of the church saw the light. The old murderer Saul was gone—now replaced by a Christ-follower, the apostle Paul. But at first no one trusted Paul enough to welcome him into the church. After all, this man had put other Christians to death.

But one of the men in the church, Barnabas, put his arm around Paul. He stuck his neck out for him, going out on a limb to welcome him into the fold, even though the other disciples were unsure (Acts 9:20-31). And you know the rest of the story. Paul went on the great missionary journeys, and many of his letters to the congregations he founded became part of the Christian Scriptures. His ministry opened the door for men and women of all races and nationalities to hear and to receive the love of Christ. What would have happened if there hadn't been a Barnabas (the name means "Son of Encouragement") in Paul's life? Thankfully, we'll never know.

winning pitch: Is there someone at school or work who needs some encouragement? Someone who is ostracized? Is there someone looking for a way into your circle of friends? Be a Barnabas. Even a Pee Wee can make a big difference in the life of someone else.

pay it forward

You then, my child, be strong in the grace that is in Christ Jesus; and what you have heard from me through many witnesses entrust to faithful people who will be able to teach others as well.
—2 Timothy 2:1-2, NRSV

"Every man on the field is charged with preserving and furthering the integrity of the game. As a player, I was responsible for holding up my end of protecting this national treasure."[1]
—Orel Hershiser, pitcher, 1983–2000

TED WILLIAMS ONCE SAID, "ALL I WANT OUT OF LIFE IS THAT WHEN I WALK DOWN the street, folks will say, 'There goes the greatest hitter who ever lived.'"[2] Ted lived up to that billing. For sheer power and average, it's hard to beat the stats of "The Splendid Splinter." His 521 home runs and a .344 lifetime average don't begin to tell the story.

Ted loved to talk hitting with anyone who would listen. He could sit for hours with younger players and discuss the intricacies of batting. The stance. The mechanics of a good swing. What a pitcher might throw in a given situation.

In fact, many hitters credited Ted with their own successes. Wade Boggs and Tony Gwynn won 13 batting titles between them, but both attributed their successes to Williams. Another Williams disciple was Pete Runnels, a teammate of Ted's from 1958–1962 with the Boston Red Sox. Runnels, a lefty, had previously tried to be a pull hitter, but Williams encouraged him to take advantage of the Green Monster in Fenway Park. He took Williams's advice and made adjustments that paid off. During those five years with the Red Sox, Runnels won two American League batting titles and narrowly missed a third, losing it on the last day of the 1958 season to . . . well . . . Ted Williams.

Every Ted must have a Pete. And every Paul needs a Timothy.

In order for the kingdom of God to spread, we are called to "pay it forward," to take the things we have learned and to entrust them to reliable persons. We are to model Christlikeness for others. And we don't have to wait until we are "experts" to do this. If we wait until we know all the answers, we'll never be able to disciple anyone.

All it takes to disciple another is to be one step ahead of them and to keep learning and growing. For the minute we stop learning, we also stop teaching.

Those reliable people we disciple should also be qualified to teach others. The goal is never to become "puffed up" with knowledge, but to become as Christlike as possible and pass that on to the next generation.

One Saturday in 1855, a young 18-year-old named Dwight Moody was working in a shoe store when his Sunday school teacher, Edward Kimball, visited him. Kimball told Moody about God's love, and Moody put aside all his previous doubts and prayed to receive Christ. In his lifetime, Moody preached on two continents and saw thousands come to know Christ.

One of those thousands was a young man named Wilbur Chapman. Though Wilbur had been raised in a religious home, he had doubts about his own standing before Christ. Moody personally counseled him, and Chapman went on to become a renowned evangelist in America, winning thousands of people to the Lord.

One day when Chapman was preaching in Chicago, the Chicago White Stockings (forerunners of the Cubs) had the day off, and a couple of the players attended the gathering. A star ballplayer by the name of Billy Sunday walked forward to commit his life to Jesus that day. Sunday became a household name in the early part of the 20th century, conducting evangelistic crusades and seeing untold numbers give control of their lives to Jesus.

During one of Billy Sunday's sermons, another young man heard the good news that God loved him, and he also prayed to receive Christ. That man,

Mordecai Ham, became an evangelist and a pastor and saw over 100,000 people choose Christ during his lifetime.

During one of Ham's crusades in North Carolina, a young man named Billy Frank attended the meeting. Although Billy insisted he would not go to hear Ham, he went one night, and then the next. That second night was the turning point not only for the young man, but for an entire nation, if not the world. For the young man who gave his heart to Jesus that night was none other than Billy Franklin Graham, who would become a great evangelist. Graham, an avid baseball fan, has counseled presidents, preached to more people than the apostle Paul, and seen millions come to faith in Christ.

All because 150 years ago one Sunday school teacher was faithful to pass on what he knew about the Lord.

So, Paul, who is your Timothy? *Pay it forward*.

winning pitch: It has been said that you can count the seeds in an apple, but only God can count the apples in a seed. Don't despair if your friends don't accept Christ immediately. Just be faithful to plant seeds and pray for them every day. God will see that they are watered and receive nourishment. The person you encourage toward a closer walk with Christ just might grow up to have a great impact on the world for the sake of the kingdom.

the best-pitched game ever

Oh, that you would rend the heavens and come down,
that the mountains would tremble before you!
As when fire sets twigs ablaze
and causes water to boil,
come down to make your name known to your enemies
and cause the nations to quake before you!
For when you did awesome things that we did not expect,
you came down, and the mountains trembled before you.
Since ancient times no one has heard,
no ear has perceived,
no eye has seen any God besides you,
who acts on behalf of those who wait for him.
You come to the help of those who gladly do right,
who remember your ways.
But when we continued to sin against them,
you were angry.

How then can we be saved?
All of us have become like one who is unclean,
and all our righteous acts are like filthy rags;
we all shrivel up like a leaf,
and like the wind our sins sweep us away.
No one calls on your name or strives to lay hold of you;
for you have hidden your face from us
and made us waste away because of our sins.
Yet, O LORD, you are our Father.
We are the clay, you are the potter;
we are all the work of your hand.
—Isaiah 64:1-8

"All I know is that we lost the game. What's so historic about that? Didn't anyone else ever lose a thirteen-inning shutout before?"[1]
—Harvey Haddix, pitcher, 1952–1965

THE SIMPLE ANSWER TO HADDIX'S QUESTION IS NO. ON MAY 26, 1959, Pittsburgh Pirate Harvey Haddix pitched what historians consider the greatest game in all of major-league history. It was at County Stadium against the Milwaukee Braves, a team with feared sluggers such as All-Stars Joe Adcock and Del Crandall, and future Hall-of-Famers Eddie Mathews and Hank Aaron.

A no-hitter is uncommon enough that it only occurs a few times each season at best. But a perfect game, where not even one of the opposing batters reaches base, is among the rarest of performances in all of baseball. And after nine innings, Harvey Haddix had pitched such a game. Not one Brave had reached base.

The problem was, the hapless Pirates were having trouble scoring against All-Star pitcher Lew Burdette. Though their lineup had managed many hits off Burdette, even one by Haddix himself, the Pirates had failed to score.

So on Haddix toiled. Through the tenth inning. Through the eleventh inning. Through the twelfth inning. 36 Braves up, 36 Braves down. No hits, no walks, no errors. Absolute perfection.

Until the thirteenth inning.

In the thirteenth, Braves infielder Felix Mantilla reached base on an error by Don Hoak, the Pirates third baseman. With the perfect game spoiled, Haddix continued to pitch with determination. Eddie Mathews sacrificed Mantilla to second. To get a chance for a double play, Haddix walked future home-run king Hank Aaron to put men on first and second. Pitching to Joe Adcock, Haddix put the second pitch into Adcock's wheelhouse and the big first baseman drove a fly into deep right-centerfield, over the wall, costing Haddix and the Pirates the game. Ultimately, the game was scored 1–0 because of a base-running error by Aaron.

But the damage was done. The most perfectly pitched game ever in history ended in a loss.

Have you ever done anything perfectly? Chances are, even at your best, there's always room for improvement. God says our very best, the highest we can attain on our own, is like a filthy rag in his sight. Imagine—the pinnacle of your achievement, the highest moral success you can attain to, the greatest standard of personal perfection, still pales in light of a holy God.

Even one sin, one mistake pitch of the heart, is enough to cause us to fall completely short of God's holiness. The good news is that we have been justified by faith through the death of Jesus, so we now have peace with God. *Justified* means "made righteous"—just as if I'd never sinned.

winning pitch: You are not perfect, and you never will be in this life. Have you asked Christ to forgive you of your sins? You can start today by acknowledging that he is the Master Potter, and you are the clay. Ask him to come down and do something awesome in your life today. Thank him for taking your imperfect life and justifying you.

the lineup card

Do not exalt yourself in the king's presence,
and do not claim a place among great men;
it is better for him to say to you, "Come up here,"
than for him to humiliate you before a nobleman.
—Proverbs 25:6-7

"My feeling is that when you're managing a baseball team, you have to pick the right people to play and then pray a lot."[1]
—Robin Roberts, pitcher, 1948–1966

BEFORE THE PLAYERS EVER GET TO THE PARK, THE MANAGER HAS BEEN AT WORK, filling out the lineup card. Some use a lot of statistics and the law of averages to determine who will play and where they will hit in the lineup. Others play a hunch, believing a player is "due" against a certain pitcher. Some never change the lineup; others change it every day.

The New York Yankees used to wear numbers on their uniforms according to where they hit in the lineup. Babe Ruth wore number three. Typically the third batter in the lineup is the best hitter on the team. By virtue of batting third, he will come to bat more than most, and if he has good "table setters" in front of him, he has the opportunity for more RBI's than most on the team.

For over 15 years in Houston, the Astros have had the "Killer B's" in Craig Biggio and Jeff Bagwell. Biggio has had an excellent on-base percentage for years, usually batting leadoff or second, and Bagwell has almost always batted third. The results have been very successful for Houston fans, as Bagwell is often among the league leaders in RBI's, and Biggio is often at the top in runs scored.

Until recently.

The aging process and a slump in statistics led a new manager to shuffle Bagwell down in the order, from hitting third, to fifth, then to sixth. This can be pretty demeaning for a player, and rumors that Jeff was washed up began to spread.

Many ballplayers would balk at being moved down in the lineup. It can hurt their statistics, which ultimately hurts their pocketbook at contract time. Many might sulk and pout, or spout off excuses to the news media, or immediately demand a trade.

But not Bagwell.

Jeff let the blame fall squarely on his shoulders (including the arthritic one) and simply said he hoped the new lineup would make the team better, adding,

"It's not about me."[2] It has always been about *the team* for Bagwell. Always quick to accept the blame for team failure, and always quick to pass on the praise for his own successes, Bagwell knows the definition of humility like few other players in the league.

Proverbs 25:6-7 reminds us that it is best to show up in the clubhouse assuming you're going to bat sixth, and then get surprised that you're hitting third. Better to do this than to expect to bat third, only to be asked to hit sixth.

Where do you bat in the everyday lineup of your life? Do you accept your position? No team ever won a game with eight players—nine are needed to play the field. The truth is, when God wants to exalt a person, he can get the job done, and he doesn't need our help.

winning pitch: Ask God to help you accept his lineup card for your life for today. God knows how the game will play out today like no one else, and his plans for your life can be trusted.

the bullpen phone

"At that time the kingdom of heaven will be like ten virgins who took their lamps and went out to meet the bridegroom. Five of them were foolish and five were wise. The foolish ones took their lamps but did not take any oil with them. The wise, however, took oil in jars along with their lamps. The bridegroom was a long time in coming, and they all became drowsy and fell asleep.

"At midnight a cry rang out: 'Here's the bridegroom! Come out to meet him!'

"Then all the virgins woke up and trimmed their lamps. The foolish ones said to the wise, 'Give us some of your oil; our lamps are going out.'

"'No,' they replied, 'there may not be enough for both us and you. Instead, go to those who sell oil and buy some for yourselves.'

"But while they were on their way to buy oil, the bridegroom arrived. The virgins who were ready went in with him to the wedding banquet. And the door was shut.

"Later the others also came. 'Sir! Sir!' they said. 'Open the door for us!'

"But he replied, 'I tell you the truth, I don't know you.'

"Therefore keep watch, because you do not know the day or the hour."
—Matthew 25:1-13

"I try to do two things: locate my fastball and change speeds. That's it. I try to keep it as simple as possible. I just throw my fastball to both sides of the plate and change speed every now and then. There is no special food or anything like that; I just try to make quality pitches and try to be prepared each time I go out there."[1]
—Greg Maddux, pitcher, 1986–present

WHEN THE PHONE RINGS IN THE BULLPEN, YOU'D BETTER BE READY. FRANK Minton remembers one relief pitcher in high school who hadn't had much playing time. On one particular off day, the young man played a round of golf without a shirt. The next day he was so sunburned he could hardly move. The thought of pulling his scratchy wool jersey across his torso was too painful to imagine, so he decided to just put his soft warm-up jacket on, confident that he would not be called upon to pitch. But his team quickly mounted a 15–0 lead, and a relief pitcher was needed for the mop-up innings. Suddenly the coach looked his way and told him to start warming up. Shock, embarrassment, and disappointment flooded the young man's face as he peeled back his jacket to reveal his sunburn to his coach. He had blown his opportunity to play.[2]

Most fans remember Robin Yount, Hall of Fame player for the Brewers. But few remember his brother, Larry Yount, who is on record as having the shortest big-league career of all. Larry was one of several September call-ups the Astros made in the waning days of the 1971 season. He had produced a solid effort at Triple-A Oklahoma City and was excited about joining the big-league team.

Unfortunately, Larry had to spend a stint in the military reserves before he could join the Astros. Too much time to kill and no throwing off a mound left him unprepared for the big leagues.

"I was just sitting around for a week and hadn't done anything," Yount remembered. "I usually had some stiffness when I had come back from other layoffs, and there was no question at the time that I had no business trying to pitch that soon. But I was a 21-year-old kid, and like any 21-year-old, I wasn't going to turn down a chance to show them what I could do. I went to the mound and took a couple of tosses, but it [his elbow] continued to hurt, so I came out," he added.[3]

Yount's name was officially entered into the game and the box score, but he never threw even one pitch. He never came back from the arm troubles and finally retired in the mid-1970s, his name the answer to the trivia question, "Who had the shortest major-league career ever?"

The challenge for relief pitchers is different than that for starters. They may hang out and laugh together for the first few innings, but the mood gets tense as the game wears on and they wait for the bullpen phone to ring.

Most of us like having plans. But we can get so caught up in our own agendas, our own schedules, that we aren't prepared when something great passes by. A relief pitcher may *plan* to get into the game, but if he isn't *prepared*, he'll miss his chance. The five unprepared bridesmaids in Matthew 25 were in the wrong place at the wrong time—trying to purchase extra oil when they should have had a supply of oil in the first place. They missed out on the coming of the Bridegroom.

Jeremiah 29:11 reminds us that God is involved in our lives: "I know the plans I have for you," declares the LORD, "plans to prosper you and not to harm you, plans to give you hope and a future." Instead of praying, "Lord, bless my plans," maybe we should ask, "Lord, what are you already doing around me? Prepare me—help me make adjustments—that I might join you in the work that you are already doing."

To be prepared is to be in the condition of the five wise bridesmaids. When a moment of greatness came their way, they were prepared—they had enough oil to light their lamps. In Scripture, oil is symbolic of the Holy Spirit. When we are filled and refilled with the power of the Holy Spirit, we will be prepared for anything.

winning pitch: We can't plan for when Jesus will return, for we don't know when that will be—but we *can* be *prepared* for his return. Until he comes, we must be about the business of being controlled by the Holy Spirit on a daily basis. Take a look at Ephesians 5:15-20, and jot down the evidences of a life that is filled with the Spirit.

PENNANT RACE

Finally, be strong in the Lord and in his mighty power. Put on the full armor of God so that you can take your stand against the devil's schemes. For our struggle is not against flesh and blood, but against the rulers, against the authorities, against the powers of this dark world and against the spiritual forces of evil in the heavenly realms. Therefore put on the full armor of God, so that when the day of evil comes, you may be able to stand your ground, and after you have done everything, to stand.
—Ephesians 6:10-13

"More [people] fail through lack of purpose than lack of talent."[1]
—Billy Sunday, outfielder, 1883–1890, and evangelist

true blue

The ear that heeds wholesome admonition
will lodge among the wise.
Those who ignore instruction despise themselves,
but those who heed admonition gain understanding.
The fear of the LORD is instruction in wisdom,
and humility goes before honor.
—Proverbs 15:31-33, NRSV

"It's the only occupation where a man has to be perfect the first day on the job and then improve over the years."[1]
—Ed Runge, American League umpire

HOW DO YOU FEEL ABOUT THE MEN IN BLUE? DO THEY EVER FRUSTRATE YOU? Ever find yourself shouting remarks about an umpire's eyesight? Would you change your tune if an umpire humbly admitted making mistakes from time to time?

"We're a necessary evil," laughs Ted Barrett, major-league baseball umpire now in his tenth season, who has been behind the plate for historic games such as David Cone's perfect game and Greg Maddux's 300th career win. "But we like to say they can't play the game without us."

Barrett, like most umpires, is an athlete. He played football in college and then went to umpiring academy. "It's tough at first," says Barrett. "Umpiring school is expensive, and the odds are low that you'll even graduate. Then the salary and travel in the low minors make it tough for you to want to stay in the profession. But it does get better, the higher up the ranks you climb."

Having come to Christ at age eight, Barrett got involved in Campus Crusade during his college years and continued to grow in Christ. Later, as an umpire, he began to develop a heart for other umpires, especially those struggling in the lower ranks. He began to attend seminary and take classes in order to better minister to the others. "I compare walking with Christ to working home plate. I'll see about 300 pitches per night, and my goal is to be perfect. But I've never walked off the field after a game and thought I had called each pitch perfectly."

What's perfect for the pitcher frustrates the hitter. What's perfect for the hitter angers the pitcher. The result is that the umpire usually hears the complaints from both sides, which is frustrating at best and infuriating at worst. At that point, an umpire must really work hard to keep his cool. "One night I was working the plate and having a difficult time maintaining self-control," remembers Barrett.

"At one point, on the last out of an inning, I lost my temper pretty bad. Chris Singleton, a strong believer in Christ, had been the runner on third base, and as he came jogging off the field, he passed by me and simply said, 'You need to honor the Father with your actions and your words.' At the time I didn't like it, but after a few innings I realized the Holy Spirit was working on me, and Chris had been right.

"Another night I was behind the plate for an American League game. The home team was at bat, and the batter lined to the shortstop. The shortstop caught the line drive, but the ball rolled out of his glove. The second base umpire didn't see it, though, and ruled it a catch. Immediately the third base coach of the team at bat began to argue with the second base umpire. When he didn't get anywhere with that, he came at me pretty hot. Again, I lost my cool with the coach and his team, and acted pretty ungodly at one point."

Over the next few days and weeks, Barrett began to feel convicted by the Holy Spirit that he had acted rashly toward the coach. "One night I was really broken about it," says Barrett. "It was as if God was saying, 'You need to make this right. I want obedience in *all* areas of your life—on *and* off the field.'

"I knew I had to apologize, but I kept waiting, thinking I would run into the coach, but that team wasn't on my schedule to umpire for quite a while. Finally I decided to call him. I explained that I had acted wrong and that it wasn't the way I wanted to act as a Christian. The coach actually didn't believe it was me at first. A major-league umpire had never apologized to him before, so he thought it was one of the coaches playing a practical joke on him.

"But later in the season I saw him at a game and spoke to him in person. It was then that he realized that it really had been me on the phone, and I had been very serious about the apology. See, among our peers, the ability to apologize is not a highly touted skill. My calling this coach on the phone to apologize would be considered taboo. But I knew it was more important to be obedient to what God was telling me to do. After all, I'd already had a reminder from the Holy Spirit through Chris Singleton that I needed to honor God with my actions."[2]

Selective obedience is really disobedience. We can't pick and choose which rebukes we will listen to. When someone draws you aside to let you know you've messed up, they're really doing you a big favor. Don't get defensive when rebuke comes. Even in the most heartless of scolding there is probably at least a grain of truth, and it's up to you to find it.

winning pitch: Here's a dangerous prayer: Ask God to put someone in your life to tell you the truth about yourself. It's easy to surround ourselves with friends and family who will let us slide. But Scripture says a wise person wants to know and understand the truth about his or her life, and that truth comes only by listening to life-giving rebuke.

a flood of forgiveness

Therefore, as God's chosen people, holy and dearly loved, clothe yourselves with compassion, kindness, humility, gentleness and patience. Bear with each other and forgive whatever grievances you may have against one another. Forgive as the Lord forgave you. And over all these virtues put on love, which binds them all together in perfect unity.

Let the peace of Christ rule in your hearts, since as members of one body you were called to peace. And be thankful. Let the word of Christ dwell in you richly as you teach and admonish one another with all wisdom, and as you sing psalms, hymns and spiritual songs with gratitude in your hearts to God. And whatever you do, whether in word or deed, do it all in the name of the Lord Jesus, giving thanks to God the Father through him.
—Colossians 3:12-17

"Whatever bitterness he was entitled to never shone through. I certainly felt he was entitled to quite a bit of it."[1]
—Giants announcer Hank Greenwald, on learning of Curt Flood's death

BY THE LATE 1950S EVERY MAJOR-LEAGUE TEAM HAD INTEGRATED AT LEAST one black ballplayer onto their roster, but the racism and bigotry of the past were far from over. Jackie Robinson had been a trailblazer, but many other African American ballplayers would also be ostracized for years to come. Curt Flood was one of these players. But an experience in the minor leagues shaped the way he saw the game and brought him to the most important choice he would ever make in his life.

"By 1957 I thought I was beyond crying," said Flood. "One day we played a doubleheader. After the first game we came into the clubhouse and put our uniforms into a big pile. The equipment manager was to clean the uniforms.

"The clubhouse attendant came to the pile with a long stick with a nail on the end, and carefully picked my uniform out from the uniforms of all the white guys. He sent my uniform to the 'colored' cleaners over twenty minutes away. So there I sat while all the rest of the team went back onto the field for the second game."

With tears in his eyes, Flood said, "I finally got my uniform and went back onto the field, where the fans had been mocking and taunting me. They called me every name in the book but a child of God."

But Curt Flood *was* a child of God, having received forgiveness for his sins by trusting that Jesus could forgive him. "I am pleased God made my skin black," Flood said later. "I only wish [God] had made it thicker." Flood could cover centerfield at the speed of light, so it seemed. He came to be regarded as one of the best defensive centerfielders in all of baseball in any era. He routinely hit over .300, stole bases, and did what it took to make the St. Louis Cardinals World Series champs in 1964 and 1967. He was also, however, routinely turned down for raises, with the racist explanation from management that "white kids require more to live on than black kids."

"I lost money, coaching jobs, and a shot at the Hall of Fame," said Flood in later years. "But when you weigh that against all the things that are really and truly important, things that are deep inside you, then I think I've succeeded."[2]

Ultimately, bitterness contaminates the vessel in which it is carried. This is a sad truth about the poison of anger. Fortunately, Curt Flood realized that we are never more like God than when we forgive. He chose to forgive those who had abused and taunted him and chose not to allow an unforgiving spirit to be a toxin in his soul. He lived in peace toward the end of his days, because even though he had been hurt greatly, he chose to forgive greatly.

This is the way God works, too. The apostle Paul said, "Where sin increased, grace increased all the more" (Romans 5:20). If there is no sin that God can't forgive, then who are we to carry grudges and hard feelings toward others? Forgive someone today. It may well be the most important decision you ever make.

winning pitch: Ask God to bring the name of someone you need to forgive to your mind today. Then take steps to contact that person and begin to make peace with him or her. You are never more like God than when you forgive.

corkboard at wrigley

For we are God's servants, working together; you are God's field, God's build-ing. According to the grace of God given to me, like a skilled master builder I laid a foundation, and someone else is building on it. Each builder must choose with care how to build on it. For no one can lay any foundation other than the one that has been laid; that foundation is Jesus Christ. Now if anyone builds on the foundation with gold, silver, precious stones, wood, hay, straw—the work of each builder will become visible, for the Day will disclose it, because it will be revealed with fire, and the fire will test what sort of work each has done. If what has been built on the foundation survives, the builder will receive a reward. If the work is burned up, the builder will suffer loss; the builder will be saved, but only as through fire.
—1 Corinthians 3:9-15, NRSV

"I was the worst hitter ever. I never even broke a bat until last year. That was backing out of the garage."[1]
—Lefty Gomez, Yankees/Senators pitcher, 1930–1943

J UNE 3, 2003, WAS MY FIRST AND ONLY TRIP TO WRIGLEY FIELD. I WAS EXCITED about finally getting to see a game in this historic stadium that was built in 1914, a hallowed place of sorts whose grass and ivy-covered outfield walls could probably tell tales of Babe Ruth and Ernie Banks and many others.

Now, as a Texan, I'm used to watching baseball in sweltering heat and high humidity. I've never watched a game and remarked, "Sure is chilly," except in the Astrodome if I was sitting too close to an air-conditioning vent.

But that night in Chicago the temperature got down to 38 degrees. People were huddled in blankets in the stands and ordering hot chocolate. (Who brings a blanket to a game and orders hot chocolate? *Smart* Cubbies fans, that's who!)

It probably would've been a miserable game to forget, had it not been for one little incident in the second inning. Cubs slugger Sammy Sosa came to bat and hit a weak ground ball in the infield as his bat shattered. He was easily thrown out at first.

Then the game was put on hold. The home plate umpire slowly walked out toward the left side of the infield, where other umpires were already gathering. They picked up pieces of the bat and examined them. They huddled and conferred. And all the time the fans in the stands were grabbing their cell phones and calling friends at home, asking them to turn on the TV to the baseball game and tell them what was happening.

Dusty Baker, the Cubs manager, came out onto the field, but he didn't put up the typical argument a manager might give. No shouting, no nose-to-nose confrontation. No kicking dirt on the plate. In fact, I didn't even know Sosa had been removed from the game until he didn't go out to play in right field the next inning. He had been tossed for using an illegal bat that had been "corked."

Of course, much has been made of the fact that Sosa's bat had been corked. Supposedly, a corked bat will allow the hitter to increase his bat speed. Sosa stated he grabbed the bat by mistake, that it was used only occasionally in batting practice to fool around with, and that he had never used it in a regular game.

A lot of people are like that bat. We may look like we have it all together on the outside, but on the inside we are not as we appear. All it takes is a 95-mile-per-hour fastball in the form of a trial or temptation to shatter the illusion that we don't have any problems internally.

What are you building your life with? A baseball bat is typically made of solid ash, hickory, or maple—some of the hardest and most solid woods on the planet. In the same way, we are called to build our lives with materials that will stand the test of time—love, faith, justice, and more.

winning pitch: Dodgers pitcher Orel Hershiser says, "The ability to honestly see yourself act, hear yourself talk, see the look on your own face, and answer the question 'What's it like to live with me?' is a very useful thing."[2] Humbly ask a trusted friend, mentor, or coach this question, and don't be defensive about the answer. Commit to listen rather than to explain and justify yourself to them. You need to know the truth about what is inside your life.

investment advice

"I tell you, use worldly wealth to gain friends for yourselves, so that when it is gone, you will be welcomed into eternal dwellings."
—Luke 16:9

"The one constant through all the years, Ray, has been baseball. America has rolled by like an army of steamrollers. It has been erased like a blackboard, rebuilt, and erased again. But baseball has marked the time. This field, this game—it's a part of our past, Ray. It reminds us of all that once was good and it could be again."[1]
—The character Terence Mann in the movie *Field of Dreams*

ONE OF THE REASONS BASEBALL HAS TRANSCENDED TIME IS ITS ABILITY TO STAY the same through the years. Grandfathers can take their grandsons to a game and know that there are still three strikes to an out, three outs to an inning, and nine innings to a game. The ball is still round and the field is still a diamond. But one thing in the game has changed radically since the 1970s—the salary of a baseball player.

From the 1920s through the 1960s, the minimum wage salary for players was about seven times the minimum wage salary in the United States. By 1967 the average major-league baseball salary was still only $19,000 a year. Today it is well over $2 million a year, making it difficult for many fans to relate to a ballplayer. And with the increase in salary come the toys—expensive sports cars, mansions, and portfolios that rival those of CEOs of major corporations. In fact, many players have a small army of agents, attorneys, and investment counselors to help them make smart decisions, and even then bad investment decisions can be made.

But some players are known for making the right kind of investments, the kind that can't be measured at Wall Street's closing bell every day. John Smoltz is just such a player.

The right-hander has been a vital cog in the Atlanta Braves staff since the late 1980s, serving as the hard-throwing contrast to finesse pitchers like Tom Glavine and Greg Maddux. Converted to the bullpen in 2001 after developing arm problems, Smoltz became a feared closer until his return to the starting rotation in 2005. Through all the changes to the vaunted pitching staff of the Braves over the last 15 years, Smoltz has been the one constant.

There is no doubt that Smoltz has done well financially, but that is not what drives him. He realizes that there are only two things a person can invest in that will pay dividends throughout eternity: the Word of God and other people.

"I realize the source of my strength. I tried to do it apart from him for a long time. I'm learning to receive God's strength and grace," says the All-Star hurler, who then cites John 15:5 as a powerful verse of Scripture he has bought stock in with his heart: "I am the vine, you are the branches," says Jesus. "Those who abide in me and I in them bear much fruit, because apart from me you can do nothing" (NRSV).

"All of this, all of the things of the world, are temporary," says Smoltz, who regularly studies the Bible along with a small cadre of committed Braves players. "The world tries to tell us that what we have down here is so good, but I am sure the rewards and joys of heaven transcend anything this world has to offer.

"I don't have to prove anything to anybody," Smoltz says with relief. "I know following Jesus works," he says, "but don't believe what I'm saying—I may fail you. Believe what the Bible says. You've got to go to the Bible."[2]

Another inside trading tip from the tall right-hander: Invest in people who need to know Christ.

One night during spring training, Smoltz rented out a movie theater in Florida and invited all his teammates to attend a private screening of the movie *The Passion of the Christ*. What would prompt someone to give away free tickets to a movie? Smoltz says, "I would like for everyone to know the joy I have known since 1995. I want to share that joy and I want to be open and unashamed about my faith, but I also realize I can't force my beliefs on others. You can't witness by thinking everyone is a nail and you are a hammer.

"It is the most defining movie for what we stand for and what we believe," Smoltz says. "I think it will continue to have a significant impact on those who see it for a long time. God's glory will shine through this movie. But the financial investment was nothing compared to the life-changing opportunities."[3]

In Luke 16:1-9, Jesus tells the story of a savvy middle-manager who cooks the books in order to prepare for his future. Jesus' praise of the manager seems odd until one understands the point: We are to invest in others so that someday we will be welcomed into heaven by those who have come to know Christ as a result of our investments.

winning pitch: Take a look at your spiritual investment portfolio today. What does the balance sheet show regarding your personal assets in God's Word? Are you bullish on the Bible? And what about your capital expenditures on behalf of other people? As Jesus goes on to say in Luke 16:13, "You cannot serve both God and Money." Which one is Lord of your life today? Wise investments in this life will reap untold wealth in the life to come.

with reverence and awe

Therefore, since we are receiving a kingdom that cannot be shaken, let us be thankful, and so worship God acceptably with reverence and awe, for our "God is a consuming fire."
—Hebrews 12:28-29

"Bob Gibson is the luckiest pitcher I ever saw. He always pitches when the other team doesn't score any runs."[1]
—Tim McCarver, catcher, 1959–1980, and baseball announcer

EVEN THE GREATEST OF PLAYERS HAVE GAMES WHERE THEY DON'T PLAY THEIR best. And if you've played for as many years as Roger "The Rocket" Clemens has, you know there are going to be some games where you go to the mound with less than your best stuff.

Such was the case one balmy night in Houston, Texas. Clemens had won over 300 games in the American League. He had been invited to his hometown of Houston to play for the Astros, in hopes of leading the team to its first World Series.

Clemens started the season on a roll, but eventually there came a night when his usual pinpoint control was failing him. Although his pitches appeared close to the strike zone, there were several that were borderline, and the umpire chose to call them balls instead of strikes.

Normally the fiery and competitive Clemens might have confronted the umpire directly to complain. Often a pitcher will stare in at the umpire if he feels that calls have not been consistent. Some have even been known to come down off the mound and yell at the ump, which usually results in getting tossed out of the game. But on this night Clemens did nothing of the kind. His catcher came out to the mound, and Clemens just looked at the ground, talking quietly. Eventually the umpire came out to the mound, where Clemens, in an obvious show of respect, continued to talk quietly, his head bowed down. Clemens was seeking clarification on the strike zone, but he didn't want to show up the home-plate umpire. The man in blue told Clemens what he was and wasn't going to call a strike. Once he had heard from the umpire, Clemens settled down for the rest of the evening and pitched a strong game, eventually getting the victory.

Hebrews 12:28-29 reminds us to "worship God acceptably with reverence and awe, for our 'God is a consuming fire.'" We are never in a position to demand an explanation from God. God is sovereign, which simply means God has "first-rights" in our lives.

Just as Clemens spoke to the umpire with his head down, preferring to ask rather than demand, so too our approach to God must be filled with reverence and awe. When was the last time you bowed your head *and* your heart in worship? When you come into God's presence, are you so filled with your own words that you can't hear God speaking? Do you think God owes you an explanation? Or do you simply and humbly acknowledge the fact that you owe God your very life?

winning pitch: Spend some time with God today completely aware of the fact that you have twice as many ears as you do mouths. Draw near to God to listen rather than to inform. Words so often fail anyway. Acknowledge your dependence upon words, and ask God to help you learn to develop a dependence upon him as you pray with reverence and awe.

yo la tengo

I have become all things to all [people] so that by all possible means I might save some.
—The apostle Paul in 1 Corinthians 9:22

"We've got to learn to stay out of triple plays."[1]
—Casey Stengel, commenting on the 1962 New York Mets

ONE OF THE MOST BASIC PRACTICES OF THE GAME IS TO "CALL IT" WHEN YOU intend to catch a fly ball. Communication between fielders is a must for a team to win. Young players are taught this from day one, but the blooper films on the sports shows prove that it is easier said than done. Take the case of the 1962 New York Mets.

The Mets were a laughable, lovable expansion team in 1962. Their record shows that they were one of the worst teams of all time, winning 40 games and losing 120. Many of the colorful, zany bunch were castoffs from other teams or young players looking to make it in the majors. Most were has-beens or never-will-be's.

Shortstop Elio Chacon was in his third and final year in the show. Hailing from Caracas, Venezuela, Chacon spoke mostly through an interpreter. Future Hall of Famer Richie Ashburn patrolled center field for the Mets, and his knowledge of Spanish was even more limited than Chacon's command of English. On pop-ups behind second base, Ashburn would yell, "I got it! I got it!" only to run dangerously close to Chacon time and again.

In an effort to shore up the defense up the middle (not to mention avoid unnecessary painful contact), Ashburn learned how to say, "I got it," in Spanish. "Yo la tengo," he learned to say, over and over. "Yo la tengo."

The next time a lazy fly ball was hit to shallow left-center, Ashburn rushed in, shouting, "Yo la tengo! Yo la tengo!" Chacon immediately recognized what Ashburn was saying and backed off as Ashburn camped under the pop-up, ready to squeeze it in his glove.

Unfortunately, left fielder and Pittsburgh native Frank Thomas (as in, *no habla español*) also rushed in and ran over Ashburn.

This is a humorous story, but it prompts the question: Do you ever struggle to communicate the gospel to others? Do you ever feel a little funny about it, like you're just not getting through? No one should have to jump through cultural hoops in order to hear and understand the story of God's love.

Everyone should be able to receive the message of grace in his or her own tongue and cultural norms.

The apostle Paul once wrote, "Though I am free and belong to no [person], I make myself a slave to everyone, to win as many as possible. . . . I have become all things to all [people] so that by all possible means I might save some. I do all this for the sake of the gospel, that I may share in its blessings" (1 Corinthians 9:19, 22-23).

winning pitch: Develop a friendship with someone who has a different racial, ethnic, national, or religious background than you do. Learn about their customs and mannerisms. For those who have not received Christ, you may well be putting your foot in the door to share God's love with them.

DOG DAYS OF SUMMER

Praise be to the God and Father of our Lord Jesus Christ! In his great mercy he has given us new birth into a living hope through the resurrection of Jesus Christ . . . until the coming of the salvation that is ready to be revealed in the last time. In this you greatly rejoice, though now for a little while you may have had to suffer grief in all kinds of trials. These have come so that your faith . . . may be proved genuine and may result in praise, glory and honor when Jesus Christ is revealed. —1 Peter 1:3-7

"The problem with being Comeback Player of the Year is it means you have to go somewhere before you can come back."[1]
—Bert Blyleven, pitcher, 1970–1992

"I think and believe that basically the one thing God expects of us is that we get up to the plate of life and swing at the ball—that we don't hide in the supposed shelter of the dugout, and that when we do go to bat, we don't stand up there with the bat on our shoulder and take strikes. At least we swing."[2] —Red Barber

the cross and the catcher

Therefore, since we are justified by faith, we have peace with God through our Lord Jesus Christ, through whom we have obtained access to this grace in which we stand; and we boast in our hope of sharing the glory of God. And not only that, but we also boast in our sufferings, knowing that suffering produces endurance, and endurance produces character, and character produces hope, and hope does not disappoint us, because God's love has been poured into our hearts through the Holy Spirit that has been given to us.
—Romans 5:1-5, NRSV

"Dad . . . can we have a catch?"[1]
—The character Ray Kinsella in the movie *Field of Dreams*

"What's important is that baseball, after 28 years of artificial turf and expansion and the designated hitter and drugs and free agency and thousand-dollar bubble gum cards, is still a gift given by fathers to sons."[2]
—Michael Chabon, Pulitzer-prize-winning author

IF THERE'S ONE THING THAT MAJOR LEAGUERS DESIRE, IT IS THAT SOMEDAY THEY will have sons who will surpass their own accomplishments and play ball even better than their fathers. And it all starts with that wonderful game of catch between father and son.

Do you remember playing catch with your father? Maybe you were amazed that he could still "bring it" after being at work all day. Perhaps you were trying to impress him with that curveball you'd been working on.

Del Crandall was a catcher, mostly for the Braves in the 1950s and 1960s. The eight-time All-Star was an integral part of the Milwaukee Braves World Series teams in 1957 and 1958. He was often considered the second-best catcher in the league, behind Roy Campanella. Crandall was also a dedicated Christian.

Dr. Jess Moody recalls that at one point in his career, Crandall was asked to speak at a Fellowship of Christian Athletes banquet on the topic "How Christ has made me a better ballplayer." Crandall turned the tables on the unsuspecting crowd, however, when he began by stating that he did not believe Christ had come to make him a better ballplayer. He believed with all his heart that God had given him raw talent but that the Lord expected him to practice, develop his skills, and hone his talent.

"What if I'm up there at bat, praying, 'Lord, help me get a hit'?" asked Crandall. "And what if the opposing pitcher is a Christian? What if he's praying, 'Lord, help me strike this guy out'? Is God flipping a coin in heaven, trying to decide whose prayer he will honor?

"There's something more at stake here. I don't believe Jesus came to make a difference in my ability to play ball," said Crandall. "But it is the dream of every ballplayer that he will have sons who will outshine him in ability, sons that will go on to play the game and do even greater things. I certainly have such dreams."

Crandall continued: "I have four sons, but two of them have mental retardation. And at least one of them will never be able to play catch with me."

He paused and then said, "And this is exactly where Jesus came to make a difference in my life—he came to help me handle my disappointments."

Tears filled the eyes of the audience as they realized they had been ministered to not merely by an All-Star ballplayer, but by a man who bore his cross as gracefully as his chest protector and mask. With a deep sense of God's purpose in his life, Crandall said, "It may be that these children were given to us because God knew we would be strong enough to take care of them."[3]

Ever been disappointed in the way your life has turned out? Anyone disappointed with God has been the victim of false teaching, because, as Romans 5 assures us, God does not disappoint.

winning pitch: What about your own letdowns? Are you learning to trust Christ with them? Share your bitter pills of disappointment with a trusted friend this week. If you're frustrated with God, admit it. Then give those disappointments over to God, so that they can be used as stepping-stones to a life of strength and character that reflects God's glory.

the tall tactician

Be completely humble and gentle; be patient, bearing with one another in love.
—Ephesians 4:2

"The value of a life is measured by its impact on other lives."[1]
—Epitaph on the tombstone of Jackie Robinson

IN THIS DAY OF FREE AGENCY, IT IS RARE FOR A PLAYER TO STAY WITH ONE TEAM during his entire career. Today's question for most well-traveled Hall of Fame players is "Which team cap will you be wearing on your plaque in Cooperstown?" There was a time in baseball, however, when players couldn't switch teams at will. Even managers had more staying power than they have today. And the granddaddy of them all was Connie Mack.

Cornelius MacGillicuddy began his playing career in 1886 and finished his baseball career as an owner in 1956 when he died. That's 70 years of baseball. He is most known for managing the Philadelphia Athletics from 1901 to 1950.

No, that is not a typo. Connie managed for 50 years.

Change? You'd better believe he saw plenty of it.

Look up the term "throwback to the old days" and you'll see that it's Connie they're talking about. When he started playing in the 19th century, organized major-league baseball allowed only white men to play. It was the era of the "dead ball," and very few home runs were hit. All games were played in the daytime and suspended if it got too dark. There was no such thing as a farm system in which players could develop through the minor leagues. The Yankees didn't even exist as a team, much less as a great American dynasty. Players didn't wear numbers on their jerseys. Connie didn't even wear a uniform while managing, preferring to wear a suit and hat while sitting on the bench.

But Connie was able to gradually change with the game. He managed the A's to nine World Series, winning five of them. He patiently rebuilt his team time and again. He managed the first All-Star game in 1937. In fact, Connie holds the record for the most wins as a manager, a record that will probably never be broken. And he had the absolute respect of everyone who ever played for him.

Oh, he was known for being a shrewd businessman, but he also had a way of discerning the measure of a person. On more than one occasion he would take a chance on a player, realizing that his job was to help develop character that could help the team win. In the 1929 World Series, Connie surprised the baseball world by using fading veteran pitcher Howard Ehmke as his starter in game one, instead of stars like Lefty Grove or George Earnshaw or Rube Walberg. Ehmke had appeared in only eleven games that whole season, but he told Mack that he had "one good game left in this arm of mine." Mack, whose nickname was "The Tall Tactician," patiently listened to Ehmke and believed him. Ehmke rewarded Mack's confidence in him by winning and setting what was then a record for most strikeouts in a World Series game.

Or take the case of another pitcher, Lou Brissie. As a young man, Lou had always wanted to pitch for the A's. After seeing him pitch, Mack agreed that the young man had talent but encouraged him to go to college first, which he did. Then came World War II, and Brissie ended up with a severely shattered leg as a result of being wounded while on patrol in Italy. Through letters, Connie encouraged Brissie to keep up his spirit, assuring him that there would be a place within the organization when he got back.

Twenty-three operations later, Brissie appeared on Mack's doorstep with an obvious bad leg but a heart full of determination. A place was found for him in the minor leagues, and it didn't take long for Brissie to show that he belonged at the major-league level. He pitched six years in the majors and even made the All-Star team before retiring. But he never would have made it that far had Connie Mack not been patient with him.

Do you ever have trouble being patient with people? It's pretty easy to write someone off as having no talent or ability, especially if all you give him or her is a quick look on the surface. But gaze deeper into the hearts of the people around you, and you'll see that they possess infinite potential to impact their world.

The earthly ministry of Jesus was short—only three years. Yet he had the opportunity time and again to have his patience tested by a group of unlikely disciples who seemed as if they would never grasp the vision of the kingdom of God. Jesus patiently worked with the disciples, loving them, nurturing them into the "All-Stars" they would later become. If he had not shown patience to impetuous Peter, or to doubting Thomas, or to renegades James and John, what would our world be like today?

winning pitch: Patience is a developed virtue—it doesn't come naturally. You'll develop your patience only by being around people who put it to the test. In those times, thank God for your increasing patience, which will yield much fruit in your dealings with others.

all-night pitcher

Consider it pure joy, my brothers, whenever you face trials of many kinds, because you know that the testing of your faith develops perseverance. Perseverance must finish its work so that you may be mature and complete, not lacking anything.
—James 1:2-4

"What you have to remember is that baseball isn't a week or a month but a season—and a season is a long time."[1]
—Chuck Tanner, manager, 1970–88

IN TODAY'S WORLD OF SET-UP MEN, SITUATIONAL LEFTIES, AND CLOSERS, A COMplete game by a starting pitcher is a rare commodity. A "quality start" is determined to be at least six innings pitched and fewer than four runs given up. But years ago, a pitcher was expected to complete most of his starts—most of the nine-inning games, anyway. Use of relievers was reserved for extra innings.

So how long would you expect a *non-pitcher* to pitch?

Odell "Red" Barbary was a catcher with a strong arm. Playing for the Charlotte Hornets of the Piedmont League in 1942, Red was a fun-loving teammate who could liven up the locker room with good-natured boastful bantering. "It's a shame talent like mine has to go to waste catching," he would often remark. "I used to be a great pitcher in my high school days."

For the last game of the season, in a time-honored tradition for teams that don't make the playoffs, the Hornets manager allowed players to choose which position they would play. With all his previous boasting, Barbary's teammates were insistent that he take the mound, and he willfully obliged them.

Red started the game with a rather awkward pitching form, and he ran into trouble in the second inning, when the opposing team scored three runs. But his own teammates rallied in the fourth inning and tied the game 3–3.

From that point on, Barbary seemed to find his stride and improve with each inning. He sailed through the fifth, sixth, seventh, eighth, and ninth innings with relative ease, keeping his team in the game by allowing no more runs. But the Hornets were having their own trouble at the plate, so at the end of nine innings of regulation play, the score was still tied 3–3.

So the game continued. The great Babe Ruth had pitched 14 innings in a World Series game in 1916. Red wasn't thinking about the Bambino, however. He kept pitching on through the 13th, 14th, 15th and 16th innings. Fine defensive plays were being made behind Barbary, and he continued to show more form and poise than he did at the beginning of the game. Fans from the community began to arrive at the ballpark to see the spectacle play out. And Red kept pitching, through the 17th, 18th, 19th, 20th, and 21st innings.

Mercifully, the game ended in the 22nd inning, when Charlotte scored a run that made Odell Barbary the winning pitcher. In the locker room after the game, Barbary confessed, "I never pitched a game before tonight in all my life!"[2]

At times you may feel that you are in the 11th inning of a 22-inning game, with no relief coming in from the bullpen. Whether it is athletic competition, the drudgery of an endless job, or a relationship that seems to have lost its purpose, we are challenged to press on and develop the staying power that will help make us complete in Christ.

Maybe you feel like you're in the midst of long project and you've never done anything like it before. That can be discouraging, even intimidating at times.

Just look over your shoulder for a moment, though, and you'll see how far you've already come. And your God has not brought you this far to abandon you. He will see you through this time. God's goal for your life is that you become mature and complete in him, and he will move heaven and earth, if necessary, to make it happen.

winning pitch: Memorize James 1:2-4. Be patient with yourself. Your loving Creator sure is.

fear at fort herrmann

He who dwells in the shelter of the Most High
will rest in the shadow of the Almighty.
I will say of the LORD, "He is my refuge and my fortress,
my God, in whom I trust."
Surely he will save you from the fowler's snare
and from the deadly pestilence.
He will cover you with his feathers,
and under his wings you will find refuge;
his faithfulness will be your shield and rampart.
You will not fear the terror of night,
nor the arrow that flies by day,
nor the pestilence that stalks in the darkness,
nor the plague that destroys at midday.
—Psalm 91:1-6

"I wasn't scared [during my first at-bat]. I just told [my teammates] to give me all that hockey equipment [forearm pad and shin guard respectively]."[1]
—Roger Clemens, pitcher, 1984–2005

WHAT COULD POSSIBLY CAUSE A BURLY MAJOR-LEAGUE CATCHER NICKNAMED "Fort Herrmann" to fear?

Ed Herrmann didn't fear blocking the plate in his eleven years as a catcher. He'd been offered over 50 scholarships to play college football. "I played like I was the middle linebacker, and the runner barreling toward home was the running back," Herrmann reminisces. "No way was he going to get that first down by touching home plate. I enjoyed the contact."

He didn't fear catching fellow Astros Larry Dierker's no-hitter in 1976 against the Cardinals. "When a guy is pitching a no-no, everybody leaves him alone on the bench. Nobody wants to mess him up. I was actually relaxed during the game—but Dierker was worried. After one out in the eighth, I went out to the mound and he said, 'This is as close as I've ever come'—so you know *he* was thinking about it."

Nor did Ed fear facing some of the best pitching of the century. Named to the American League All-Star Team with the White Sox in 1974, Ed says, "Oh, Jim Palmer could make you look stupid enough. He'd pitch 'backwards' or opposite the way others would pitch, by keeping you off balance, and leave you guessing what he was going to throw next. Everybody knew he had a great fastball, curve, and change-up, but you'd look silly trying to hit against him."

Herrmann didn't even fear catching some of the best pitchers the game had to offer in the 1960s and 1970s. "J.R. Richard's fastball moved so much it could really make me look pretty bad when I was behind the plate. But I'd already caught the knuckleball from Hoyt Wilhelm [Hall of Famer] and Wilbur Wood [20-game winner four years in a row] with the White Sox, so I was used to it."

No, the greatest fear Ed Herrmann ever had to conquer didn't come until after his playing days were over. "I come from a line of ballplayers," he says. "My grandfather was with Brooklyn in the National League in 1918 [a team that featured future Hall of Famers Zack Wheat, Burleigh Grimes, and Rube Marquard]. My dad would've played baseball except for World War II. He always warned me to not let baseball run my life. But when you are young, it really engulfs you.

"Some of my fear was that I would not succeed, that I would disappoint the fans or my teammates. But when my dad passed away in 1991, my real fears began. It was frightening to know that the one person I had depended on all my life was gone. He had been a rock for me, and I had to find somebody to replace him.

"I turned to Jesus and invited him into my life. That and the truth of God's Word have replaced all my fear."[2]

Have you suffered a loss recently? Is there a void in your life that makes you feel wobbly or shaky? Anxiety disorders may disrupt our living, and fear may come and go, but the calm presence of Christ can still even the most frightened heart and give you a firm place to stand.

winning pitch: On a sheet of paper, list the five things that you fear most. Write Psalm 91 in big letters over the fears, and then ask God to fill you with an inner strength to stare down the fears every day. You might be surprised in a year to look back at the page and realize most of your worst anxieties never materialized.

the phenom

Do your best to present yourself to God as one approved by him, a worker who has no need to be ashamed, rightly explaining the word of truth.
—2 Timothy 2:15, NRSV

"Son, what kind of a pitch would you like to miss?"[1]
—Dizzy Dean, pitcher, 1930–1941

THE WORD *PHENOM* HAS COME TO MEAN IN BASEBALL WHAT *PRODIGY* MEANS in music: a young, highly talented person capable of performing on a level far beyond their years. And pitcher David Clyde was the phenom of phenoms.

In his senior year in high school, David went 18–0 with five no-hitters, allowing only three earned runs in 148 innings. The fledgling Texas Rangers franchise made him their number one draft pick in 1973, gave him a very large bonus, and saw a chance to build their crowds by having the young native of Houston, Texas, jump directly to the majors from high school.

Baseball is unique among other sports in that it utilizes a minor league system where young players can hone their skills and receive instruction. The average major-league player spends at least three years in various levels of the minors before he gets his first cup of coffee in the show. Only a fortunate few have made a successful jump from high school to the majors without playing in the minor leagues.

Unfortunately, David Clyde's leap was not that successful.

Oh, his major-league debut was pretty exciting, all right. He received a good-luck telegram from Sandy Koufax before the game, and in front of a sellout crowd, he pitched five innings and got a win against the Minnesota Twins, striking out the side in the first inning he ever pitched in the big leagues.

But the unrealistic expectations grew after the game. One man can't save a struggling team. Clyde was in the pressure cooker with no mentors, no training on how to face seasoned veteran major-league batters instead of fuzzy-cheeked high school kids, and no personal guide on how to live life. "The correlation I felt was like going from high school to performing open-heart surgery," Clyde once said. "I felt that's how much better I had to be."[2]

Eventually, he injured his arm, and his career lasted only five years in the big leagues, during which he compiled an 18–33 record. Today his name is synonymous with how *not* to develop a young pitcher. No team wants to make the same mistake that the Rangers made with David Clyde. God does have a purpose for your life and that call is always first a call to preparation. Even the "superheroes" of the faith had to go through times of training and education, and they needed to gain experience before they were able to be used greatly by God.

Some may assume that the apostle Paul, after having his Damascus road experience (Acts 9), immediately went on all the missionary journeys, wrote his letters that became books of the New Testament, and became a superstar apostle overnight. Not so. In Galatians, Paul talks about a period of over three years and then another period of 14 years that occurred before much of his public ministry began. What do you suppose Paul was doing during that time? Training. Learning. Growing.

Growth is time-consuming, at least for things worthwhile. You can grow a majestic oak tree in 50 years, or you can grow a squash plant in six weeks. Both are beneficial, but which one will have the most impact for the longest time? One of the qualifications for the Baseball Hall of Fame is that a player have an outstanding career over a span of many years, not just one flash-in-the-pan season.

So don't get discouraged if you feel you've not yet accomplished God's plan for your life. Just continue to take the time to prepare for it. It will eventually come, and it will be even more satisfying than you can dream.

winning pitch: Are you ready to handle God's Word? Do you consistently study the Bible in depth, or are you content to let your pastor break it open for you only once a week? Get involved in a small group that meets regularly and dive into God's Word with them.

winners never quit

When Jesus had received the drink, he said, "It is finished." Then he bowed his head and gave up his spirit.
—John 19:30, NRSV

"Winners never quit, and quitters never win."[1]
—George Steinbrenner, Yankees owner

THE BASEBALL HALL OF FAME IN COOPERSTOWN, NEW YORK, HOLDS AN INDUCtion ceremony every year, during which a few players are added to its enshrined ranks. In their induction speeches, players usually thank a variety of people who have helped them through the years.

Coaches, teammates, and family members all play a part in helping develop a Hall of Fame player. But the game, which is so much fun to play for kids, has a funny way of chewing up and spitting out those who give their lives to it.

"I was ready to quit," says John Boccabella, now retired 31 years from the game. "I had been a backup my whole career, and wasn't playing very well, so I really thought it was time."

Boccabella had come up with the Cubs in 1963 as a first baseman and occasional outfielder, and then he was converted to catcher by manager Leo Durocher in 1966. But the Cubs already had All-Star Randy Hundley blocking the plate, so for six years Boccabella spent time with both the parent club and their AAA affiliate.

In 1969 major league baseball was expanding into Montreal and San Diego, and the Expos selected Boccabella in the expansion draft. "I was excited to go somewhere where I could play more, but I soon realized that Ron Brand and John Bateman would be handling most of the catching duties. In 1969 I only got into 40 games and hit .105, so I thought, 'Here I go again.'

"At the end of 1972, I had played four years with the Expos, and I was still never really anything but the backup catcher, so I decided I'd had enough. After ten years in the big leagues, I was still making the minimum salary for a ballplayer, so I came home to California on the promise of a job with the utility company. Around the 20th of December, I received another standard contract from the Expos, the same [salary] as the year before. It confirmed my decision to me: 'I'm glad I'm quitting.'

"But during the winter they had gotten rid of John Bateman and their other catchers. A few days later the GM called and said they wanted to give me a raise to sign, but I told them I was still going to retire. Two days later he called back and offered me an additional raise, but I told him my mind was made up. Then a friend of mine told me I was crazy, so a few days later I called the Expos back and they talked me into it.

"I went to spring training in 1973 as the number one catcher in camp. They assigned me, a ten-year veteran catcher, to room with rookie catcher Gary Carter. He was a real excitable powerhouse kid, and it was obvious he was something special as a ballplayer. We became good friends and spent many nights talking about the game and about catching. We also talked a lot about the Lord and Scripture. I told him, 'Gary, someday you are going to be a big star in baseball and bring a lot of people to Jesus. He's going to direct your life, and you're going to give him all the credit."[2]

Carter picks up the story from here: "When I graduated from high school, I was drafted by the Montreal Expos. After a year of rookie ball, I went to my first major league training camp, and my roommate that spring was John Boccabella.

"John was a catcher like myself. He'd had a lot of major league experience, and he taught me a lot. But the thing that stands out most about him, that has affected me more than anything else I've learned in baseball, was that John was a Christian. And he wasn't afraid to tell me about it. . . .

"Through John, I learned what it really meant to be a Christian. I saw that God didn't hate me or have anything against me. On the contrary, He loved me very much. When I understood that, I asked Jesus Christ to come into my life."[3]

And because John Boccabella didn't quit, he had the best season of his career in 1973. He also had a big impact on Gary Carter, who went on to star for the Expos and Mets. Thirty years after John almost quit baseball, he saw Carter inducted into the Hall of Fame as one of the best catchers ever to play the game. And in Carter's induction speech, John saw his prediction for Gary come true. Gary said, "Above all, I want to thank my Lord and Savior, Jesus Christ. A great verse that spoke to me while writing my speech, and kind of explains what it is all about, comes in Psalm 18: 'I love you, LORD; you are my strength. The LORD is my rock, my fortress, and my savior; my God is my rock, in whom I find protection. He is my shield, the strength of my salvation, and my stronghold. I will call on the LORD, who is worthy of praise' [vv.1-3 NLT]. I praise the Lord, my God, my best friend, for giving me the ability, the desire, the love, and the guidance that brought me here today. Without you, I would be nothing."[4]

Don't quit. Someday there will be an induction into God's Hall of Fame, the new heaven and earth, when we will thank the Lord for his great sacrifice at the cross. For without Jesus, we are truly nothing. And God's purpose for your life just might be that you contribute to the success of others, so that one day someone in heaven will be there because you didn't quit.

winning pitch: Who in your circle of friends needs to know of your faith in Christ? Don't give up. There is a Gary Carter who needs you to hold on a little longer, pray a little harder, and give a little more. You just might get to see him in God's Hall of Fame someday.

OCTOBER GLORY

This is how we know that we love the children of God: by loving God and carrying out his commands. This is love for God: to obey his commands. And his commands are not burdensome, for everyone born of God overcomes the world. This is the victory that has overcome the world, even our faith. Who is it that overcomes the world? Only he who believes that Jesus is the Son of God.
1 John 5:2-5 (NIV)

"Please don't interrupt me, because you haven't heard this one before: The Brooklyn Dodgers, champions of the Baseball World . . . honest."[1]
—*Washington Post* reporter Shirley Povich, October 5, 1955

"This is the last pure place where Americans dream. This is the last great arena, the last green arena, where everybody can learn the lessons of life."[2]
—Marcus Giamatti, quoting his late father, Bart Giamatti, baseball executive

we are family

*Just as each of us has one body with many members, and these members do
not all have the same function, so in Christ we who are many form one body,
and each member belongs to all the others.*
—Romans 12:4-5

"Awards mean a lot, but they don't say it all. The people in baseball mean more
to me than statistics."[1]
—Ernie Banks, Cubs infielder, 1954–1971

THROUGH THE YEARS, A FEW TEAMS HAVE STUCK AROUND LONG ENOUGH AND
been successful enough to be referred to by another nickname in addition
to the name of their mascot. Say "Bronx Bombers" and one immediately thinks
of the Yankees. "Big Red Machine" refers to Cincinnati's strong team of the
1970s; "The Amazing Mets" are the 1969 World Series champs; and "Harvey's
Wallbangers" are the Milwaukee Brewers of the early 1980s.

Only one team is referred to by the name of a popular song: the Pittsburgh Pirates of "We Are Family" fame of 1979. The song, originally recorded by the disco group Sister Sledge, had a short shelf life, but the team it came to describe is still talked about today as a unique group of players who came together at just the right time to win a championship.

They were an oddball group of young players and veteran castoffs who came from different backgrounds, and all had different roles. There were "Pops" Stargell, "Scrapiron" Garner, "Cobra" Parker, "Mad Dog" Madlock, and "Candy Man" Candelaria.

The Pirates were careful to reward their teammates with a gold star for the hat when someone did something good on the field. And always, in the locker room, the song "We Are Family" could be heard playing.

First baseman Willie Stargell was the leader of the team, and he was the National League MVP that season. Third baseman Bill Madlock came over in a midseason trade and batted .328 the rest of the year. John Candelaria and Bruce Kison were pitchers known for winning key ball games down the stretch. And reliever Kent Tekulve was "lights out" with 31 saves.

Getting hot at just the right time, the 1979 Pirates won the National League East Division by two games, swept the "Big Red Machine" in the playoffs, then came from behind three games to one to eventually overtake the heavily favored Baltimore Orioles in the World Series, a feat accomplished by only six teams in history. As long as baseball is played, the "We Are Family" Pirates will be remembered.

The song "We Are Family" should be played not only in the clubhouse, but also in the church house. After all, the church is made up of brothers and sisters in Christ (Matthew 12:50).

The church has many members, but they all form one body (Romans 12:4-5). Some are infielders and some are pitchers. Some bat cleanup and some leadoff. Some are utility players; others are left-handed specialists. Some are visible on the All-Star team, and some are pinch hitters. Some are black, some are white, some are Asian, and some are Latino. But *all* are equal in God's sight, and *all* are important if a team is to succeed.

Maybe you've been burned by a church experience. Perhaps something happened that turned you off to joining in worship with and studying alongside other Christians. Maybe you're one of those who mutters "The church is full of hypocrites, so I won't participate." But the church is still the tool that God is using to reach a lost world. And you can help make the church faithful to that call, if you choose to.

Hey, Ruth had Gehrig; Mantle had Maris; Biggio has Bagwell. No one can carry a team by himself or herself. A team is made up of 25 players at a time, chosen from a 40-man roster. For a team to win, *each* member has to accept the role assigned by the manager.

Are you committed to a local church? Not merely as a member on paper, but are you a participating part of the body of Christ? The "We" in "We Are Family" is big enough to include you—are you big enough to include them?

winning pitch: If you're already an active member of a local congregation, thank God for that church, and pray for its leaders every day. If you aren't a part of a local church, begin to pray and ask for God's direction. He will surely direct you to a team that needs your abilities and gifts.

dream pursuit

[*Jesus*] *came to a town in Samaria called Sychar, near the plot of ground Jacob had given to his son Joseph. Jacob's well was there, and Jesus, tired as he was from the journey, sat down by the well. It was about the sixth hour.*

When a Samaritan woman came to draw water, Jesus said to her, "Will you give me a drink?" (His disciples had gone into the town to buy food.)

The Samaritan woman said to him, "You are a Jew and I am a Samaritan woman. How can you ask me for a drink?" (For Jews do not associate with Samaritans.)

Jesus answered her, "If you knew the gift of God and who it is that asks you for a drink, you would have asked him and he would have given you living water."

"Sir," the woman said, "you have nothing to draw with and the well is deep. Where can you get this living water? Are you greater than our father Jacob, who gave us the well . . . ?"

Jesus answered, "Everyone who drinks this water will be thirsty again, but whoever drinks the water I give [them] will never thirst. Indeed, the water I give [them] will become in [them] a spring of water welling up to eternal life."

The woman said to him, "Sir, give me this water so that I won't get thirsty and have to keep coming here to draw water."
—John 4:5-15

"You see, you spend a good piece of your life gripping a baseball, and in the end it turns out that it was the other way around all the time."[1]
—Jim Bouton, pitcher, 1962–1970

IT IS THE DREAM OF VIRTUALLY EVERY LITTLE LEAGUER WHO HAS EVER PLAYED THE game. Deep down inside, we all long to be the hero who hits the two-out home run in the World Series, the one who comes through in the clutch, the one who saves the day. And Bernie Carbo fulfilled that dream. But it didn't take him long to realize that the dream didn't fulfill him.

Bernie was in the major leagues for 12 years and was known as "the best 10th man in baseball." He was the first player drafted by the Cincinnati Reds in the first ever major league baseball draft in 1965, and he was chosen as *The Sporting News* Rookie of the Year in 1970, batting .310 with 21 home runs.

By 1975 Bernie had been traded to the Red Sox, and he was instrumental in one of the greatest games ever played. The World Series that year pitted the Red Sox against Bernie's former team, the Reds. In game six, with the Reds leading the Series 3–2, Bernie was sent up to pinch-hit in a do-or-die situation. With 2 outs and two men on base in the bottom of the 8th inning, Bernie hit a clutch home run to tie the game. The Red Sox went on to win in the 12th inning with the famous walk-off home run waved out of the park by Carlton Fisk.

After all those years of playing the game he loved, Bernie's dream came true. He was on top of the world, a true baseball hero. Replays showed his home run over and over. Reporters lined up at his locker to interview him. His name was splashed across newspaper headlines the next day. And how long did the great feeling last?

"I woke up the next morning depressed," says Bernie, now manager of an independent league team. "My initial thoughts were, 'How am I going to top that? What do I have to do today in order to please everybody?' I woke up the next morning not even wanting to go to the ballpark for game seven."

Bernie knocked around from team to team, becoming known as a solid utility player but never finding as much success as he had in Boston. "I got caught up in believing that being a professional baseball player and making a lot of money and having a family and being in the paper would fulfill me, but I was really just looking for acceptance, wanting people to like me and be there for me. It eventually led to drug and alcohol abuse. I realize now that God wants to fill those needs."[2]

In our search for a meaningful life, we often seek that which cannot satisfy. We often try to draw water from dry wells. The wells of popularity, accomplishment, addiction, financial success, and earthly praise will never satisfy the deepest longings of the human heart. Jesus says to us as he said to the Samaritan woman, "Put your bucket down in me. I alone have that which will fulfill you."

winning pitch: Memorize John 10:10, which says, "The thief comes only to steal and kill and destroy; I have come that they may have life, and have it to the full." Don't let the thief steal your joy—ask God to fill your bucket today with living water. God is the only one who can satisfy your soul.

the scapegoat

"When Aaron has finished making atonement for the Most Holy Place, the Tent of Meeting and the altar, he shall present the live goat. He is to lay both hands on the head of the live goat and confess over it all the wickedness and rebellion of the Israelites—all their sins—and put them on the goat's head. . . . The goat will carry on itself all their sins to a solitary place; and the man shall release it in the desert."
—Leviticus 16:20-22

"[Shoeless Joe] Jackson's fall from grace is one of the real tragedies of baseball. I always thought he was more sinned against than sinning."[1]
—Connie Mack, Philadelphia A's owner and manager, 1901–1950

"SHOELESS JOE" JACKSON IS, QUITE SIMPLY, THE BEST BALLPLAYER WHO EVER lived who is not enshrined in the Baseball Hall of Fame. His life is the stuff of legends. It is said that Babe Ruth copied his swing, that Joe slept with his bat "Black Betsy," and that his glove was the place "where triples go to die."

He earned his nickname as a player in the minor leagues when he played an entire game in his socks, because his new spikes were too tight. Jackson remains the only player to hit over .400 in his rookie season, and his lifetime batting average is .356, second only to Ty Cobb.

In 1919 Jackson played for the Chicago White Sox. The team was owned by Charles Comiskey, a tightfisted businessman with a reputation for underpaying his players, reneging on promised bonuses, and even charging them for cleaning their uniforms. Toward the end of the season, when it became apparent that Chicago would face Cincinnati in the World Series, gamblers approached certain players about the possibility of throwing the games for profit. It wasn't difficult to find players who were frustrated with Comiskey. Seven men agreed to the terms. Jackson was also approached with a bribe, but he refused to take any money, though the gamblers assumed that he was in on the fix. Jackson reportedly went to Comiskey with the information but was rebuffed.

During the Series, which Chicago lost five games to three, it became obvious to many that several on the Chicago team were making halfhearted efforts and playing sloppily. Not Jackson, however. He hit .375 for the Series and played well in the outfield. But in the end, he was accused with the other seven players, because he had known about the efforts to throw the games.

The damage to the game was done. Baseball's reputation was quickly falling. In an effort to seek redemption from the fans, the owners appointed Judge

Kennesaw Mountain Landis to become the first commissioner of baseball. "Baseball is something more than a game to an American boy," said Landis. "It is his training field for life work. Destroy his faith in its squareness and honesty and you have destroyed something more; you have planted suspicion of all things in his heart."[2]

"Baseball had been polluted and rendered unclean by the scandal," wrote William Herzog. "Some ritual was needed to restore the purity of the sport."[3] To restore that purity, Landis banished the accused White Sox (now commonly called the "Black Sox") from ever playing major league baseball again. Fair or not, Jackson was exiled from baseball, and with it his chances of being elected to the Hall of Fame disappeared. From time to time it was said that he would be found playing on some semi-pro team, but never again did he play in the majors.

In Leviticus 16 God gave the Israelites instructions for observing a Day of Atonement. The word *atone* means "to cover", and in this way the people would know that their sins had been covered over. The priest was to take two male goats for this sin offering. One would be sacrificed, its blood shed, symbolizing the price to be paid for their sin. The other goat was the scapegoat. The priest would symbolically put his hands on the head of the goat, confess all the sins of the people, and transfer all the wickedness to the goat. Then the goat would be sent away into the wilderness, banished forever. This would symbolize the removal of sin and its guilt.

Joe Jackson was the scapegoat for baseball for many years. Though it was never proved that he had done wrong, the sins of baseball were transferred onto his head, and he was banished into the wilderness. In this way baseball could go on, redeemed and restored.[4]

In an infinitely greater way, Jesus is our scapegoat. At the cross, all of our sins were laid upon him. Our guilt and shame were not only covered over; our sins were put away as if they had never been committed.

The story of legend goes that when Jackson departed from the courthouse after the trial, a boy in the crowd came up to him and said, "Say it ain't so, Joe." For those who hear for the first time the story of God's redemption through his Son, the plea is more like "Say it *is* so—tell me my past is forgiven."

winning pitch: Why not observe your own day of atonement this week? In Jewish tradition, the day is often observed with fasting and prayer, and emphasis is placed on confession of sin and repentance. It is a day to ask forgiveness for promises broken to God. Thank Jesus for being your scapegoat, the one who has covered all your sins.

what game are you watching?

Therefore, since we are surrounded by such a great cloud of witnesses, . . . let us run with perseverance the race marked out for us. Let us fix our eyes on Jesus, the author and perfecter of our faith, who for the joy set before him endured the cross, scorning its shame, and sat down at the right hand of the throne of God. Consider him who endured such opposition from sinful men, so that you will not grow weary and lose heart.
—Hebrews 12:1-3

"When the One Great Scorer comes to write against your name—He marks not that you won or lost but how you played the game."[1]
—Grantland Rice

OCTOBER 10, 2004, WAS A UNIQUE DAY FOR SPORTS HISTORY IN HOUSTON, Texas. That day, four major sporting events were being played across the city. The Houston Astros were fighting to win a playoff game against the

Atlanta Braves. Across town, the Houston Texans were competing against the Oakland Raiders. A few hours later, the Houston Rockets would play a preseason game in their new arena, and the last round of a Champions Tour golf tournament was winding down at Augusta Pines.

Some fans had tickets to more than one event, and spent part of the afternoon traveling from one game to another. But almost all were concerned for the Astros, who were in a must-win game. It became apparent during the Texans' game that many fans had brought portable radios to the game and were watching the Texans but listening to the Astros. The crowd occasionally cheered when there wasn't anything to cheer about on the field in front of them. And at the golf tournament, fans would circulate the score of the ball game quietly so as not to distract the players on the course.

It is easy to get so focused on the game of life immediately in front of us that we miss the bigger picture. Sometimes the daily commute means work is an hour down a congested freeway to a gray-walled cubicle in a skyscraper. Sometimes it means a thankless trip up a staircase with one more laundry basket in tow. Either way, it is easy to miss the little victories that come our way every day. A smile from a reluctant colleague at the water cooler. A toddler's first prayer. Some days it seems all you can do is just tie a knot in the rope and hang on for dear life, especially when the game in front of you seems to be going the way of the opposition.

But Scripture calls us to walk by faith, not by sight. When we keep our eyes (and our ears) on Jesus, he gives us the perspective to be able to look at our apparent defeats and struggles and still rejoice because of the ultimate victory that he provides. The scoreboard may say one thing, but the one we listen to says another.

Hebrews 12:2 says, "Let us fix our eyes on Jesus, the author and perfecter of our faith." When we are looking to Jesus and listening to him, we won't find that we suffer fewer defeats. But we *do* find that he will be with us to sustain us during our defeats.

winning pitch: Call your mind back to attention at regular points during the day. Focus on the truth of ultimate victory in Christ, and ask the Holy Spirit to help you rejoice even during trials.

dropping the ball

This is the message we have heard from him and proclaim to you, that God is light and in him there is no darkness at all. If we say that we have fellowship with him while we are walking in darkness, we lie and do not do what is true; but if we walk in the light as he himself is in the light, we have fellowship with one another, and the blood of Jesus his Son cleanses us from all sin. If we say that we have no sin, we deceive ourselves, and the truth is not in us. If we confess our sins, he who is faithful and just will forgive us our sins and cleanse us from all unrighteousness. If we say that we have not sinned, we make him a liar, and his word is not in us.
—1 John 1:5-10, NRSV

"The condemned jumped out of the chair and electrocuted the warden."[1]
—A baseball writer after seeing catcher Mickey Owen's gaffe in the
1941 World Series

THINK OF ALL THE MOMENTS THAT DEFINE A CAREER IN BASEBALL. MICKEY Owen had plenty of them. He hit the first pinch-hit home run in an All-Star game in 1942 at the Polo Grounds. He is one of only three people to hit a game-ending grand slam. And he set the National League catcher's record of 476 consecutive errorless chances accepted, setting a Dodger season record by fielding .995. Unfortunately, Mickey is remembered for one thing: the day he dropped the ball.

It was game four of the 1941 World Series between the Brooklyn Dodgers and the New York Yankees. The Dodgers were winning the game 4–3 in the ninth inning, about to tie the Series at two games apiece. With two outs and a 3–2 count on Yankee Tommy Henrich, the game was all but over. Dodger pitcher Hugh Casey threw a sharp-breaking curveball, and Henrich missed for strike three.

But the ball got away from Owen. And if the catcher drops strike three, the batter can run to first base, which Henrich did safely. The Yankees then sent a slew of hitters to the plate in an unbelievable 11th-hour rally and won the game 7–4. They went on to win the next day, too, ending the Dodgers' hopes for their first World Championship.

The fans and the newspapers jumped all over Owen. A now-famous picture shows Owen scrambling for the ball and Henrich looking over his shoulder as he runs to first base. Owen blamed himself for the loss. "I don't mind being the goat," he said. "I'm just sorry for what I cost the other guys."[2] Still, the Dodgers had hit only .182 in the Series, not exactly dominating the Yankee pitching.

But Mickey Owen refused to let that one failure define his life. "The missed third strike, instead of ruining my career, will make me a better catcher . . . until the day I hang up my glove and mask forever," he said in a 1942 interview,[3] and he was right. He played big league baseball for 13 years, after which he coached and scouted. He later founded the Mickey Owen Baseball School in Missouri, one of the most successful training schools ever. He became sheriff of Green County, Missouri, and held the post for over 15 years, serving his community well. He also became an elder in his church near Springfield, Missouri, and lived a life of service to God. On top of all this, he remained in great shape and was still playing in old-timers' games in his seventies.

Sometimes it is more difficult to forgive ourselves than it is to forgive others. Our enemy loves to accuse us and remind us of our past failures, discouraging us from ever trying to live for Christ. Someone once said, "When Satan reminds you of your past, just remind him of his future!"

Sure, you've dropped the ball. Join the club. All of us have.

Our world is not looking for someone who is perfect, who never makes a mistake. Who could relate to such a person? Our world is looking for someone who, after they have fallen, still finds a reason for hope and forgiveness and gets back up to face another day. Jesus gives us that forgiveness when we simply ask him for it.

C'mon, the game of life's not over. The faithful will win. Get back in the game, like Mickey did.

winning pitch: If a sense of guilt and shame continues to cloud your heart, try this little exercise. On a piece of paper, write down every sin you can think of that you have committed. Then with a large marker, write 1 John 1:9 over the top of the list. Thank God that every one of your sins—past, present, and future—is forgiven. Then throw the list away and go face the day together with your Savior.

in the bag

"Where, O death, is your victory? Where, O death, is your sting?"

The sting of death is sin, and the power of sin is the law. But thanks be to God! He gives us the victory through our Lord Jesus Christ.

Therefore, my dear brothers, stand firm. Let nothing move you. Always give yourselves fully to the work of the Lord, because you know that your labor in the Lord is not in vain.

—1 Corinthians 15:55-58

"Let's hear it for a loaf of Brett, a slice of Biancalana and a pound of Balboni."[1]
—Thomas Boswell, *Washington Post* columnist

J IM SUNDBERG MADE A NAME FOR HIMSELF AS AN ALL-STAR FOR THE TEXAS Rangers in the 1970s and early 1980s, racking up a then-record six Gold Gloves as a catcher. But by 1985 he was with the Kansas City Royals, a strong club led by players such as Bret Saberhagen, Frank White, Dan Quisenberry,

Steve Balboni, and George Brett. After winning the American League West, they fought back from a three-games-to-one deficit to beat the Blue Jays in the American League Championship Series and advance to the World Series for the second time in club history.

Then in the "Heartland" World Series against the St. Louis Cardinals, the Royals found themselves in a familiar three games to one hole. Rookie Danny Jackson bailed them out in game five with a complete game. Then in game six Sundberg scored the winning run in the bottom of the ninth inning in a nail-biting 2–1 victory. The stage was set for a classic seventh game showdown.

"The odd thing is, I had told my wife, Janet, on the afternoon before that evening's game seven, I had a real sense that it was going to be a blowout," recalls Sundberg, now in the front office of the Texas Rangers. "But I didn't know which way it would be, so I was anxious about that. Well, by the fifth inning we were ahead 11–0, which is the way it would finish. And so we started celebrating privately. Bret Saberhagen was our starting pitcher, and I had told the guys that if we scored even one run, we were going to win. With an 11–0 lead, the tension was beginning to release. We were giggling and running up into the locker room to celebrate during those last four innings—we couldn't help ourselves. We knew that no one was going to come back and beat us.

"Now, we knew we had an adversary, and we knew that he would still be looking for cracks and we couldn't let our guard down. We still had to keep our nose to the grindstone. But I draw a parallel to the Christian life at this point: *How differently you live when you know victory is yours, when you know it's in the bag.*[2]

The final words of Jesus at the cross were "It is finished" (John 19:30). The "it" applies to several facts: Jesus' earthly life and ministry were finished; the road to salvation for all who believe was complete; and the defeat of evil was final. Oh, we will continue to have skirmishes, like soldiers on an outlying island who continue to fight against the enemy because they haven't yet heard the news that the war is over.

But if Jesus' earthly life and ministry are finished, that means you don't have to run out and find another hero, another savior—all you need you can find in Jesus. If the road to salvation is complete, you can finally give up trying to earn or keep your salvation through good works. And if evil is defeated, then you never need to fear again. Continue to stand firm and let nothing move you from your commitment to Christ. Victory is yours—it's in the bag!

winning pitch: Have you had a victory celebration in your life lately? Think back to the last World Series winners. How did they celebrate on the field after the final out? If they can celebrate a world championship with such emotion and exuberance, how much *more* should a Christian be able to celebrate our victory through Christ? Turn your next worship experience with other believers into a mutual victory celebration.

THE LONG WINTER

The grass withers, the flower fades;
but the word of our God will stand forever.
—Isaiah 40:8, NRSV

"People ask me what I do in winter when there's no baseball. I'll tell you what I do. I stare out the window and wait for spring."[1]
—Rogers Hornsby, Hall of Fame infielder, 1915–1937

"It's designed to break your heart. The game begins in the spring, when everything else begins again, and it blossoms in the summer, filling the afternoons and evenings, and then as soon as the chill rains come, it stops and leaves you to face the fall alone. You count on it, you rely on it to buffer the passage of time, to keep the memory of sunshine and high skies alive, and then, just when the days are all twilight, when you need it most, it stops."[2]
—A. Bartlett Giamatti, baseball commissioner

right on time

There is a time for everything,
and a season for every activity under heaven:
a time to be born and a time to die,
a time to plant and a time to uproot,
a time to kill and a time to heal,
a time to tear down and a time to build,
a time to weep and a time to laugh,
a time to mourn and a time to dance,
a time to scatter stones and a time to gather them,
a time to embrace and a time to refrain,
a time to search and a time to give up,
a time to keep and a time to throw away,
a time to tear and a time to mend,
a time to be silent and a time to speak,
a time to love and a time to hate,
a time for war and a time for peace.

What does the worker gain from his toil? I have seen the burden God has laid on men. He has made everything beautiful in its time. He has also set eternity in the hearts of men; yet they cannot fathom what God has done from beginning to end.
—Ecclesiastes 3:1–11

"[Buck O'Neil's] life reflects the past and contains many of the bitter experiences that our country reserved to men of his color, but there is no bitterness in him; it's not so much that he put that suffering behind him as that he has brought gold and light out of bitterness and despair, loneliness and suffering. He knows that he can go farther with generosity and kindness than with anger and hate."[1]
—Ken Burns, filmmaker

MUCH OF THE COUNTRY FELL IN LOVE WITH BUCK O'NEIL WHEN HE WAS INTER-viewed for the Ken Burns *Baseball* television series. O'Neil, now in his nineties, was full of wonderful stories and anecdotes about the game he so passionately loves.

In his autobiography, Buck O'Neil tells of being a black man who played professional baseball before African Americans were allowed to play in the all-white major leagues. An excellent clutch hitter and first baseman, O'Neil was an All-Star in the Negro Leagues in the early 1940s, and he even won a batting title. But by the time the color barrier was broken in 1947, O'Neil was considered too old to play in the big leagues, as were most of his teammates. Many of his friends grew bitter about their missed opportunities. O'Neil wrote: "Back in 1981, at a reunion of us Negro league players in Ashland, Kentucky, a reporter from *Sports Illustrated* asked me if I had any regrets, coming along as I did before Jackie Robinson integrated the major leagues. And this is what I told him then: . . . Waste no tears for me. I didn't come along too early—I was right on time. You see, I don't have a bitter story. I truly believe I have been blessed."[2]

The title of O'Neil's book reflects his cheerful optimism and his belief in the sovereignty of God. Despite missing fame and fortune, O'Neil chose to title his autobiography *I Was Right on Time.*

Jeremiah 29:11 says, "'For I know the plans I have for you,'" declares the LORD, "'plans to prosper you and not to harm you, plans to give you hope and a future.'" The good news is that God's plans for your life can be trusted, even though they may not turn out the way you think they should. They are plans always made in perfect love and perfect wisdom. God is never late in doing what is promised. God is always right on time.

winning pitch: Ask God today to help you trust in divine timing for your life and ask for wisdom to see divine guidance in the midst of your circumstances.

death on the diamond

As he went along, he saw a man blind from birth. His disciples asked him, "Rabbi, who sinned, this man or his parents, that he was born blind?"

"Neither this man nor his parents sinned," said Jesus, "but this happened so that the work of God might be displayed in his life."
—John 9:1-3

"You can learn a little from victory. You can learn everything from defeat."[1]
—Christy Mathewson, Hall of Fame pitcher, 1900–1916

S AY HEY. SIX-SIXTY. THE CATCH. MENTION ANY OF THESE TWO-WORD PHRASES TO a baseball fan, and one name immediately comes to mind. This Hall of Famer was in a league of his own for the better part of the 1950s and 1960s, and he is arguably the best center fielder the game has ever known. The name Willie Mays is recognized by even the most casual of fans as being synonymous with excellence and excitement.

But before Willie broke in with the Giants in 1951, the name Mays was synonymous with tragedy.

Carl Mays (no relation to Willie) was a tough, submariner pitcher whose lifetime stats are worthy of attention from those who would send players to enshrinement at Cooperstown: 207 wins, including 20 with three different teams; a lifetime .622 winning percentage; and winner of two games in the 1918 World Series. Mays even pitched both games of a doubleheader in 1918 and won them both.

But Carl Mays is remembered for something completely different.

It was August 16, 1920, and the Yankees were playing the Indians, who were led by future Hall of Famer Tris Speaker. The shortstop for the Indians, Ray Chapman, was having the best year of his career, batting over .300 and fielding flawlessly. Chapman led off the fifth inning, crowding the plate, even though Mays was known to pitch inside. Mays delivered one of his submarine pitches, and Chapman froze. He may have never seen the ball, or he may have assumed it would curve back over the plate.

It didn't. The pitch hit him squarely on the side of the head, and he crumpled at the plate. He was rushed to the hospital and died hours later.

Had Chapman been playing 60 years later, he probably would have simply had a Richter-scale headache the next day. But basic game equipment had not evolved in 1920 to include the use of batting helmets.

And it raises the question for the ages: Why do bad things happen to good people? Chapman hadn't done anything to Mays. (And there was no evidence that Mays was trying to hurt Chapman, either.)

There are no pat answers for this question. And when someone is suffering, as Chapman's widow did for many years after, easy explanations seem cold and shallow.

Jesus was asked this question in a roundabout way. In his time, it was assumed that bad things happened to people as a result of sin. Jesus was asked about a man who was blind, "Who sinned—this man or his parents— that he should be born blind?"

"Neither," said Jesus. "This happened so that God's glory might be revealed."

Some would argue that God is all-powerful but that God must not be very loving to allow pain and suffering in the world. Others would say that God is indeed love but that he is not all-powerful and thus cannot do anything about the problem of evil in the world.

But there is a third possibility, and it is this: God *is* all-powerful, and God *is* love. God doesn't want evil and suffering to rule, and he *does* do something about it.

God stands with those who suffer.

The issue is not *if* you will suffer, but *when* you will suffer. In a fallen world, pain and suffering are a part of life. Jesus promised to be with us *as* we suffer, strengthening us and giving us courage in the midst of our pain. Jesus can do this because he's got "street cred" on suffering—he's been there personally.

winning pitch: Encourage those around you today who are going through suffering and pain. Offer no easy, quick answers, but quietly and confidently show them your willingness to be a friend with them in the midst of their struggles. Remember, they can't identify with someone who never has problems or difficulties. You'll be a picture of Jesus that they can actually touch.

how long, o lord?

How long, O LORD? Will you forget me forever?
How long will you hide your face from me?
How long must I wrestle with my thoughts
and every day have sorrow in my heart?
How long will my enemy triumph over me?

Look on me and answer, O LORD my God.
Give light to my eyes, or I will sleep in death;
my enemy will say, "I have overcome him,"
and my foes will rejoice when I fall.

But I trust in your unfailing love;
my heart rejoices in your salvation.
I will sing to the LORD,
for he has been good to me.
—Psalm 13

"The talk of curses is really silly. There was no curse on this franchise. What got Boston its first World Series title since 1918 was incredible starting pitching, the best they've ever had in their history."[1]
—Peter Gammons, ESPN baseball analyst

"Now the 1918 jokes are done. Now TV networks can't ruin our playoff games anymore. Now we can watch Red Sox games without waiting for the Other Shoe. Now we don't have to deal with manipulative books and documentaries, or hear about Buckner, Zimmer, Grady, Pesky, Torrez, Stanley and Schiraldi ever again. It's a clean slate. We're like those ugly contestants who show up on "The Swan," get fifty grand worth of plastic surgery, then start sobbing in front of a full-length mirror when they see themselves. That's every Red Sox fan right now."[2]
—Bill Simmons, ESPN baseball analyst

UNTIL OCTOBER 2004, IT HAD BEEN 31,458 DAYS SINCE THE BOSTON RED SOX had won the World Series. In 1918, when they last won the world championship, penicillin had not been discovered, women couldn't vote, and the National Football League and National Basketball Association didn't even exist. The average Red Sox fan could read about the team in the *Boston Globe* newspaper, which cost 2 cents. The all-time record for home runs in a career was 138 by Roger Connor. The Red Sox pitching rotation featured a starter who was nicknamed "Babe" because he was so young. And on some off days when he wasn't pitching, the team would put him in the outfield, because he was a strong hitter. Yes, life was good in 1918 for Red Sox Nation.

But after the 1919 season, Red Sox owner Harry Frazee sold Babe Ruth's contract to the New York Yankees. And then from 1920 to 2003, the Yankees appeared in 39 World Series, winning 26 of them. During that same time span, the Red Sox appeared in only four World Series, losing all of them, giving rise to the lore of the "Curse of the Bambino." And the Red Sox/Yankee rivalry became second in history only to the Israelites and the Philistines.

Superstition aside, the Red Sox had their chances through the years. In 1946 it was Enos "Country" Slaughter's mad dash from first to home that did them in. In 1967 the "Impossible Dream" team ran into Hall of Famer Bob Gibson. In 1975 it was a heartbreaking game seven loss to the Reds; in 1978 it was Bucky Dent's home run that put the Yankees over the Red Sox in the playoffs; and in 1986 the agonizing replays of Bill Buckner's error at first base had Red Sox fans crying out, "How long, O Lord?"

King David wrestled with this very same question in a much more serious vein. In Psalm 13 he describes how he feels that God has forgotten him and that his enemy has triumphed over him. There are those who claim Christians should not have any negative thoughts, should not "question" God, and should not verbalize doubts. Yet the Psalms reveal that even the giants of the faith struggled with doubt and despair. And when they did, they didn't try to cover it up or put a happy face on their problems. They simply cried out to God everything that was on their hearts. They would "sing the blues" and desperately admit that if God didn't step in, they wouldn't make it another day.

God is big enough to handle our doubts and fears, our questions, our cries of heartache and sorrow. It is doubtful (even impossible!) that we can ask a question of God that will somehow break the back of Christianity. The Psalms reveal God's promise to be with us at all times and in all places.

The Red Sox fans made it through their dry spell. The team won another world championship in 2004, some 86 years after their last one. You can be assured that as you trust in God's unfailing love and presence, you will make it through the dry periods of your life.

winning pitch: Psalm 13:6 says, "I will sing to the LORD, for he has been good to me." Make a list today of the ways that God has been good to you, and then sing one of your favorite songs of worship. God's not interested in whether your voice sounds good as you sing. God listens to your heart.

the auction

Once you were alienated from God and were enemies in your minds because of your evil behavior. But now he has reconciled you by Christ's physical body through death to present you holy in his sight, without blemish and free from accusation—if you continue in your faith, established and firm, not moved from the hope held out in the gospel. This is the gospel that you heard and that has been proclaimed to every creature under heaven, and of which I, Paul, have become a servant.
—Colossians 1:21-23

"I feel we're all overpaid. Every professional athlete is overpaid. I got a phenomenal contract—much more money than I ever thought I'd make. I wouldn't say I'm embarrassed by it, but deep down I know I'm not worth it. To my shame, though, I have to admit I asked for it."[1]
—Fred Patek, infielder, 1968–1981

HOW MUCH WOULD YOU PAY FOR . . . A BASEBALL GLOVE? A BATHROBE? A FISH-ing rod and reel? A razor and shaving mug?

What if you were told the glove was game-used by the pitcher with the most wins of all time, Cy Young? Or that Babe Ruth used to sit around in the robe and eat way too many hot dogs? Or that Lou Gehrig used the rod and reel to catch fish when he wasn't catching throws at first base from the rest of the infield? Or that the shaving mug was used each morning by a driven man with a glint in his eye, the man who retired with the highest lifetime batting average, Ty Cobb?

Would that make a difference in what you might expect to pay for these ordinary items?

A few years ago Barry Halper, baseball collector extraordinaire, sold many of his holdings at auction. Cy Young's baseball glove sold for $71,250. Babe Ruth's lounging robe sold for $25,300. Lou Gehrig's rod and reel went for $10,350. And Ty Cobb's razor and shaving mug went for $4,025.

Collectors snatched these items up at unheard-of prices, not because the buyers needed another razor or rod and reel. No, these and many other items at auction were considered valuable because of whom they belonged to.

Sometimes we tend to compare our lives to one another using the world's economy. The bottom line on the paycheck, the late-model car, the home in the gated community. There's nothing inherently wrong with any of these things.

But if we pursue them simply so that we can gain the approval of others, we have bigger problems.

Ultimately, our value is not in what we can do or in what we own. It is not in our position or our prestige, not in our fame and fortune. It is not in gaining approval from others so that we can feel good about ourselves. Our value is simply in *whose* we are.

As a Christ-follower, you have been bought with a price. You are not your own. You belong to someone else (1 Corinthians 6:19-20). God has redeemed you and called you by name (Isaiah 43:1). Christ has reconciled you to God, and you stand before him without accusation (Colossians 1:22). Granting to others the power to determine our value would be like saying that our ability to please others is of greater worth than the blood of Christ, which paid for our sins.

winning pitch: Read 1 Corinthians 13, replacing the word "love" with "my Father." You might even memorize it this way. And the next time your self-worth is called into question, remember that you are a person of infinite worth because of whose child you are.

never too late

Jesus continued: "There was a man who had two sons. The younger one said to his father, 'Father, give me my share of the estate.' So he divided his property between them.

"Not long after that, the younger son got together all he had, set off for a distant country and there squandered his wealth in wild living. After he had spent everything, there was a severe famine in that whole country, and he began to be in need. So he went and hired himself out to a citizen of that country, who sent him to his fields to feed pigs. He longed to fill his stomach with the pods that the pigs were eating, but no one gave him anything.

"When he came to his senses, he said, 'How many of my father's hired men have food to spare, and here I am starving to death! I will set out and go back to my father and say to him: Father, I have sinned against heaven and against you. I am no longer worthy to be called your son; make me like one of your hired men.' So he got up and went to his father.

"But while he was still a long way off, his father saw him and was filled with compassion for him; he ran to his son, threw his arms around him and kissed him.

"The son said to him, 'Father, I have sinned against heaven and against you. I am no longer worthy to be called your son.'

"But the father said to his servants, 'Quick! Bring the best robe and put it on him. Put a ring on his finger and sandals on his feet. Bring the fattened calf and kill it. Let's have a feast and celebrate. For this son of mine was dead and is alive again; he was lost and is found.' So they began to celebrate."
—Luke 15:11-24

"Well, baseball was my whole life. Nothing's ever been as fun as baseball."[1]
—Mickey Mantle, Yankees outfielder, 1951–1968

THE YOUNG MAN WAS FAST. WHEN HE BURST ON THE SCENE IN 1951, IT WAS obvious he was the heir apparent to the Yankees centerfield position held by Joe DiMaggio. "Joltin' Joe" was in the waning days of a Hall of Fame career, but he didn't have the blinding speed this young man had in the field.

The young man ran and ran. He ran from the lead mines of Oklahoma to the lights of stardom in New York City.

He ran down uncatchable balls in centerfield and caught them. He stole bases. He turned singles into doubles and doubles into triples. The young man kept running. He ran from the fear of an early death, such as took his father, uncles, and grandfather. He ran toward alcohol to numb his pain and anxiety. He ran from faithfulness to his wife and children, and he ran toward a self-destructive lifestyle of seeking pleasure where he could find it.

He ran toward Cooperstown and made it easily, even when his battered legs failed him. He retired with 536 home runs, three Most Valuable Player awards, a Triple Crown in 1956, seven world championships, and the title of being the greatest switch-hitter the game has ever known. And after his career was over, Mickey Mantle kept running. He ran from God as fast and as far as he could. But by 1995 the run had slowed to a crawl: Mantle was diagnosed with cancer in his liver.

He received a liver transplant, but it wasn't long before doctors determined that the cancer had aggressively spread to other parts of his body. They told Mantle that he was not going to be able to win this race, no matter how fast he ran. So Mantle picked up the telephone and called an old teammate of his, Yankee second baseman Bobby Richardson, and talked and prayed with him. Richardson comforted Mantle with Scripture and words of encouragement.

When the world learned of Mantle's plight, fans longed for a glimpse of their hero. Mantle obliged them by holding a press conference in which he showed some of the greatest courage and humility an athlete has ever shown. His body a shell of its former self, his voice cracking, Mantle went before the cameras and declared, "Don't be like me. I'm no role model."

Weeks later, with Mantle on his deathbed, Richardson visited his old friend in the hospital. With tears in his eyes, Richardson leaned over the bed and said, "Mickey, I love you, and I want you to spend eternity in heaven with me." Mantle responded with the words Richardson had waited many years to hear: "Bobby, I've been wanting to tell you that I have trusted Jesus Christ as my Savior."[2] Mantle then quoted John 3:16, which says, "For God so loved the world that he gave his one and only Son, that whoever believes in him shall not perish but have eternal life."

Have you been running from Someone? Maybe even deep in your heart you know you'll never be fast enough to outrun the one who loves you so much that he gave his life for you. If the Father watched from a long way off and ran down the road to meet the prodigal son, God is no doubt watching you for any sign that you may come back to him. And no matter how fast you run, God can run faster to meet up with you. God will receive you no matter what you've done or how long you've been gone. All that matters is that you come home.

winning pitch: If you've never invited Jesus to be the Lord of your life, you can do it right now. If you already have a relationship with Jesus, why not search your heart to see if there's anyone you've given up on, believing they would never come to Christ. It's never too late. They may be ready to take that first step toward Jesus, if they sense from you there's always room for one more in the kingdom.

notes

spring training
1. Quoted in W. P. Kinsella, ed., *Diamonds Forever: Reflections from the Field, the Dugout and the Bleachers* (Toronto: HarperCollins Publishers Ltd., 1997), 73.
2. Richard H. Durbin, address to the U.S. House of Representatives, 1989, http://www.webball.com/skill/batsafety.html.

scout's honor
1. Quoted in Armand Eisen, *Play Ball! Quotes on America's Favorite Pastime* (Kansas City: Andrews and McMeel, 1995), 23.
2. Frank Minton, interview by Hugh Poland, digital media, Houston, Texas, 16 November 16, 2004.

hitting the cutoff man
1. Quoted in Armand Eisen, *Play Ball! Quotes on America's Favorite Pastime* (Kansas City: Andrews and McMeel, 1995), 62.

2. Alvin Dark, interview by Hugh Poland, author's notes, Easley, South Carolina, October 12, 2004.

know the signs

1. Quoted in Larry Stone, "Sign Language: The Art of Baseball Communication," *Baseball Digest*, August 2003. http://www.findarticles.com/p/articles/mi_m0FCI/is_8_62/ai_104362915/

2. Quoted in Ibid.

3. Ibid.

4. Ibid.

sacrifice play

1. Red Barber, *Show Me the Way to Go Home* (Philadelphia: Westminster Press, 1971), 153.

2. Quoted in Armand Eisen, *Play Ball! Quotes on America's Favorite Pastime* (Kansas City: Andrews and McMeel, 1995), 132.

3. Sal Bando, interview by Hugh Poland, digital media, Hartland, Wisconsin, October 6, 2004.

laughter at vinegar bend

1. Quoted in "Profile of Vinegar Bend Mizell," *Baseball Almanac*, http://www.baseball-almanac.com/players/player.php?p=mizelvi01.

2. Wilmer Mizell, interview by Hugh Poland, author's notes, Corpus Christi, Texas, 1994.

prayer locker

1. Quoted in Dave Branon and Joe Pellegrino, *Safe at Home* (Chicago: Moody Press, 1992), 201.

2. Tom Griffin, interview by Hugh Poland, author's notes, Poway, California, December 14, 2004.

opening day

1. Quoted in Armand Eisen, *Play Ball! Quotes on America's Favorite Pastime* (Kansas City: Andrews and McMeel, 1995), 36.

the heart of a pee wee

1. Quoted in Armand Eisen, *Play Ball! Quotes on America's Favorite Pastime* (Kansas City: Andrews and McMeel, 1995), 78.

2. Quoted in Dave Kindred, "Pee Wee: Spirit of a Hero," *The Sporting News*, August 23, 1999.

pay it forward
1. Orel Hershiser, *Between the Lines: Nine Principles to Live By* (New York: Warner Books, 2001), 146.
2. Quoted in Bert Randolph Sugar, *The Book of Sports Quotes* (New York: Quick Fox, 1979), 90.

the best-pitched game ever
1. Quoted in Paul Dickson, *Baseball's Greatest Quotations* (New York: HarperCollins, 1991), 172.

the lineup card
1. Quoted in Glenn Liebman, *Grand Slams! The Ultimate Collection of Baseball's Best Quips, Quotes, and Cutting Remarks* (Chicago: Contemporary Books, 2001), 137.
2. Quoted in Richard Justice, "Now Here's a Thought: Bags at No. 2," *Houston Chronicle*, June 26, 2004.

the bullpen phone
1. "Quotations from and about Greg Maddux," *Baseball Almanac*,
http://www.baseball-almanac.com/quotes/greg_maddux_quotes.shtml.
2. Quoted in Frank D. Minton, *Baseball's Sermon on the Mound* (Nashville: Broadman Press, 1976), 20–22.
3. Quoted in "Whatever Happened to Larry Yount?" *Astros Magazine*, April 1989.

pennant race
1. Billy Sunday, http://www.brainyquote.com/quotes/authors/b/billy_sunday .html.

true blue

1. Quoted in Armand Eisen, *Play Ball! Quotes on America's Favorite Pastime* (Kansas City: Andrews and McMeel, 1995), 187.

2. Ted Barrett, interview by Hugh Poland, author's notes, Gilbert, Arizona, December 1, 2004.

a flood of forgiveness

1. Quoted in Henry Schulman, *San Francisco Examiner*, January 21, 1997.

2. Quoted in *Baseball: Inning Eight, A Whole New Ballgame*, 16 mm, 120 min. (Walpole, N.H.: Florentine Films, 1994).

corkboard at wrigley

1. Quoted in Armand Eisen, *Play Ball! Quotes on America's Favorite Pastime* (Kansas City: Andrews and McMeel, 1995), 66.

2. Orel Hershiser, *Between the Lines: Nine Principles to Live By* (New York: Warner Books, 2001), 67.

investment advice

1. *Field of Dreams*, VHS, directed by phil Alden Robinson, (Dyersville, Iowa: Universal Studios, 1987).

2. Quoted in J. Gerald Harris, "'05 Braves Marked by Men of Faith," *BP Sports*, May 2, 2005 http://www.bpsports.net/bpsports.asp?ID=4975.

3. Quoted in Tim Ellsworth, "Major League Players Use 'Passion' as Outreach" (Nashville: Baptist Press Sports, April 12, 2004) http://www.bpsports.net/bpsports.asp?ID=4474.

with reverence and awe

1. Quoted in Armand Eisen, *Play Ball! Quotes on America's Favorite Pastime* (Kansas City: Andrews and McMeel, 1995), 186.

yo la tengo
1. Quoted in Bert Randolph Sugar, *The Book of Sports Quotes* (New York: Quick Fox, 1979), 7.

dog days of summer
1. Quoted in Sean Holtz, "Quotations from and about Bert Blyleven,"
http://baseball-almanac.com/quotes/bert_blyleven_quotes.shtml.
2. Red Barber, *Show Me the Way to Go Home* (Philadelphia: Westminster Press, 1971), 151.

the cross and the catcher
1. *Field of Dreams*, VHS, directed by Phil Alden Robinson, Universal Studios, (Dyersville, Iowa: 1987).
2. Michael Chabon, "It's in the Cards," *The New York Times Magazine*, July 21, 1991, 38.
3. Dr. Jess Moody, interview by Hugh Poland, author's notes, Glorieta, New Mexico, 2004. In a separate correspondence with Hugh Poland, Del Crandall corroborated the story and gave his permission to publish the story.

the tall tactician
1. Epitaph on the tombstone of Jackie Robinson,
http://www.umass.edu/umassmag/archives/1998/spring_98/spg98_f_jr.html.

all-night pitcher
1. Quoted in Paul Dickson, *Baseball's Greatest Quotations* (New York: HarperCollins, 1991), 433.
2. Betty Barbary, interview by Hugh Poland, author's notes, Simpsonville, South Carolina, 2004.

fear at fort herrmann
1. Quoted in Sean Holtz, "Quotations from and about Roger Clemens,"
http://baseball-almanac.com/quotes/roger_clemens_quotes.shtml.

2. Ed Herrmann, interview by Hugh Poland, author's notes, Poway, California, October 5, 2004.

the phenom
1. Quoted in Paul Dickson, *Baseball's Greatest Quotations* (New York: HarperCollins, 1991), 107.
2. Quoted in Kyle Ringo, "Turn Back the Block," *Baseball Digest*, August 2003.

winners never quit
1. Quoted in Dave Buscema, "Boss Stages Surreal Pep Rally," Record Online, September 2, 2004, http://www.recordonline.com/archive/2004/09/02/mlbbusc0.htm.
2. John Boccabella, interview by Hugh Poland, digital media, San Rafael, California, November 30, 2004.
3. Gary Carter, "Gary Carter," http://www.thegoal.com.
4. Gary Carter, "Text of 2003 Hall of Fame Inductee Gary Carter's Speech," Cooperstown, New York, July 27, 2003, http://www.baseballhalloffame.org/ hof_weekend/2003/speeches/carter.htm.

october glory
1. Shirley Povich, "John Podres Shuts Out Straining Yanks, 2–0," *Washington Post and Times-Herald*, October 5, 1955.
2. Quoted in Armand Eisen, *Play Ball! Quotes on America's Favorite Pastime* (Kansas City: Andrews and McMeel, 1995), 279.

we are family
1. "Ernie Banks Quotes," http://en.thinkexist.com/quotes/ernie_banks.

dream pursuit
1. Quoted in Paul Dickson, *Baseball's Greatest Quotations* (New York: HarperCollins, 1991), 55.
2. Bernie Carbo, interview by Hugh Poland, digital media, Theodore, Alabama, December 9, 2004.

the scapegoat

1. "Quotations from and about Shoeless Joe Jackson," *Baseball Almanac*, http://www.baseball-almanac.com/quotes/quojcks.shtml.

2. Quoted in William R. Herzog II, "Scapegoat to Icon: The Strange Journey of Shoeless Joe Jackson," in *The Faith of Fifty Million: Baseball, Religion, and American Culture*, ed. Christopher H. Evans and William R. Herzog II (Louisville: Westminster John Knox Press, 2002), 140.

3. Ibid., 129.

4. Ibid.

what game are you watching?

1. Quoted in Bert Randolph Sugar, *The Book of Sports Quotes* (New York: Quick Fox, 1979), 82.

dropping the ball

1. Quoted in Mike Phillips, "Bums Were Left Bumming in 1941," *Miami Herald*, October 23, 2003.

2. Quoted in David Menary, "Mickey Owen . . . in Canada?" http://www.baseballlibrary.com/baseballlibrary/submit/Menary_David1.stm.

3. Ibid.

in the bag

1. Thomas Boswell, *The Heart of the Order* (New York: Doubleday, 1989), 143.

2. Jim Sundberg, interview by Hugh Poland, digital media, Arlington, Texas, November 17, 2004.

the long winter

1. Quoted in Paul Dickson, *Baseball's Greatest Quotations* (New York: HarperCollins, 1991), 189.

2. Quoted in Armand Eisen, *Play Ball! Quotes on America's Favorite Pastime* (Kansas City: Andrews and McMeel, 1995), 79.

right on time
1. Ken Burns, foreword to *I Was Right on Time: My Journey from the Negro Leagues to the Majors*, by Buck O'Neil, with Steve Wulf and David Conrads (New York: Fireside, 1997), xii.
2. Ibid., 3.

death on the diamond
1. Quoted in Paul Dickson, *Baseball's Greatest Quotations* (New York: HarperCollins, 1991), 276.

how long, o lord?
1. Peter Gammons, "Nirvana in New England," October 27, 2004,
http://sports.espn.go.com/mlb/gammons/story?id=1910902.
2. Bill Simmons, "The Nation's Destination: Destiny," *ESPN Page 2*, October 28, 2004,
http://proxy.espn.go.com/espn/page2/story?page=simmons/041028.

the auction
1. Quoted in Paul Dickson, *Baseball's Greatest Quotations* (New York: HarperCollins, 1991), 336.

never too late
1. Quoted in Armand Eisen, *Play Ball! Quotes on America's Favorite Pastime* (Kansas City: Andrews and McMeel, 1995), 34.
2. Quoted in Ed Cheek, *Mickey Mantle: His Final Inning* (Garland, Tex.: American Tract Society, 1995).

select name and subject index

index of scriptures